We Slaves of Suriname

We Slaves of Suriname

Anton de Kom

Translated by David McKay

polity

This publication has been made possible with financial support from the Dutch Foundation for Literature. The publisher gratefully acknowledges the support of the Dutch Foundation for Literature.

N **ederlands**
letterenfonds
dutch foundation
for literature

Polity Press
65 Bridge Street
Cambridge CB2 1UR, UK

Polity Press
101 Station Landing
Suite 300
Medford, MA 02155, USA

ISBN-13: 978-1-5095-4901-6 (hardback)
ISBN-13: 978-1-5095-4902-3 (paperback)

A catalogue record for this book is available from the British Library.

Library of Congress Control Number: 2021942476

Typeset in 11 on 13 pt Sabon
by Fakenham Prepress Solutions, Fakenham, Norfolk NR21 8NL
Printed and bound in Great Britain by TJ Books Ltd, Padstow, Cornwall

The publisher has used its best endeavors to ensure that the URLs for external websites referred to in this book are correct and active at the time of going to press. However, the publisher has no responsibility for the websites and can make no guarantee that a site will remain live or that the content is or will remain appropriate.

For further information on Polity, visit our website: politybooks.com

Contents

Contents

Translator's Note

Warning: This note mentions denigrating terms that express racist attitudes and may offend or upset some readers.

Although De Kom's writing was in many respects ahead of its time, he uses terms for race and skin color that now seem quite dated and may occasionally confuse today's readers. Rather than forcing him into a twenty-first-century mold, I have looked to English-language writing of the 1920s and 1930s for equivalents: books by Richard Wright, Zora Neale Hurston, and C.L.R. James.

These authors use the term "Indian" to refer to the indigenous peoples of both the Americas and the Indian subcontinent. Adjectives are often used to disambiguate, e.g. "Red Indian" and "British Indian." (The term "West Indian," used for all inhabitants of the West Indies regardless of race, adds another degree of complexity in James's writings.) De Kom refers to the indigenous peoples of South America simply as "Indianen," rendered here as "Indians," or by terms such as "inheemsen" ("natives" or "indigenous people"), or often by the names of their specific peoples. He refers to the people of British India and the Surinamese people descended from them as "Brits-Indiërs" ("British Indians"), "Hindoestanen" ("Hindustanis"), and in two places "Hindoes" ("Hindus").

Like Wright, Hurston, and James, De Kom is sparing in his use of capital letters in terms for race and skin color, using lower-case letters for the equivalents of "black," "white," "colored," "maroon," and "creole." I have followed his example. De Kom also writes the Dutch term "neger" with a lower-case letter, but I translate this as "Negro" with a capital "N," after my English-language models. This reflects the pride and self-respect with which De Kom uses the term "neger" and the distinct contrast with the highly offensive term "nikker" (rendered as "nigger"), which he reserves for expressions of the racism of the typical white colonist. "Neger" has become such a fraught term in contemporary Dutch that De Kom's use of the word can be confusing or upsetting to twenty-first-century readers. "Negro" is actually less problematic in this respect; although it is now outdated, it is not generally seen as a term of abuse. In the introductions, the slightly different capitalization conventions reflect authorial preference and contemporary usage.

Some literary translators and other writers have recently argued that the use of italics for words regarded as foreign is an inherently racist or chauvinist practice, in that by drawing and emphasizing an absolute distinction between the native and the foreign, it reinforces invidious notions of cultural, national, and racial purity. I believe the intent and effect of this conventional use of italics vary from writer to writer and from book to book, but there can be no doubt that De Kom generally avoids italicizing "foreign" words, especially words from the Sranantongo language, and that this choice emphasizes the integrity of his distinctively Surinamese idiom. I have done the same in English but included a glossary of Surinamese terms in the back of the book, so that readers unfamiliar with Sranantongo and Surinamese idiom can better follow De Kom's vivid descriptions of his country. Where Sranantongo or other foreign terms are glossed in the main body of the book, the glosses were introduced by De Kom. I have adopted modern Sranantongo spelling throughout the book (with the indispensable aid of Professor Michiel van Kempen), both for the sake of readers familiar with Sranantongo and to improve readability and usability for readers who do not speak the language but might wish to learn more. I hope De Kom would have approved of this choice and felt, as I do, that it disentangles his work from the spelling conventions of the Dutch colonial power.

When De Kom first published his book, it was not edited to today's professional standards, and Dutch editions up to the present day have remained largely unchanged in this respect. De Kom was a political activist and a writer rather than a professional historian, and his access to research materials was severely limited; he had to rely heavily on a few main sources, mostly secondary works that quoted at length from primary sources. For these reasons, some proper names and titles contain obvious errors, and many names are given only in part (often the surname only). While this is not a critical or scholarly edition, I have attempted, with much-valued assistance from Professor G.J. Oostindie and Professor Van Kempen, to correct such errors and fill in missing names where possible. No doubt some errors remain, and I apologize for any that I have unintentionally introduced.

De Kom included both a scholarly apparatus of endnotes and a few footnotes defining terms or offering additional context. In this edition, his two sets of notes have been merged into a single series of endnotes. I have added a number of translator's notes, often intended to clarify cultural references that might otherwise puzzle modern English-speaking readers; these too can be found among the endnotes, marked with "Translator's note" or "TN."

I am grateful to Professors Oostindie and Van Kempen, David Colmer, Professor Gloria Wekker, Dr. Duco van Oostrom, Tessa Leuwsha, and Lucelle Pardoe for their insightful input, which made a tremendous difference to the final version. My thanks also to the Dutch publisher Atlas Contact, particularly Hayo Deinum, for taking the initiative for an English-language edition, to Mireille Berman and others at the Dutch Foundation for Literature for their financial and institutional support for the project, and to Elise Heslinga, John Thompson, Susan Beer, Evie Deavall, and their colleagues at Polity Press for publishing this English-language edition and giving me the opportunity to translate it. I was very fortunate to be in the right position at the right time to translate this book for publication; others who have done much more than I to promote De Kom's legacy, such as Professor Oostindie and Dr. Karwan Fatah-Black, deserve special mention here. Finally, a generous 2021 ICM Global South Translation Fellowship award from the Institute for Comparative Modernities at Cornell University enabled me to devote additional time to the daunting task of writing a translation worthy of De Kom's landmark book.

Introductions

Introduction

Frimangron

Tessa Leuwsha

I am in the Frimangron district of Paramaribo, standing in front of the birthplace of Anton de Kom. It's a corner building. On the sidewalk in front of the house is a memorial stone with a quotation from the famed Surinamese resistance leader: "Sranan, my fatherland, one day I hope to see you again. The day all your misery has been wiped away." Less than fifteen feet behind the stone, the two-story wooden house looks broken down. Drab vertical beams hang askew from nails, and part of the zinc roof has caved in. One window shutter is open, a curtain pulled aside; this is still someone's home. Beside it, a plantain tree half-conceals the low house next door. Down the walkway between the two homes, a skinny black man comes out of the backyard. His hair and beard are gray. His T-shirt is too big for him; so are his flip-flops. Holding a flower rolled up in newspaper, he sits down on the stoop in front of the former De Kom family home. I'm curious who the flower is for. He pays no attention to me – so many people take photos here.

In the 1930s, hundreds of people stood waiting here to speak to Anton de Kom. Many were unemployed; others were workers struggling to survive on meager wages. After the abolition of slavery in 1863, the Dutch authorities had rounded up indentured workers in what were then British

India and the Dutch East Indies to work on the plantations of Suriname. Later, when the agricultural economy went into decline, those workers had followed in the footsteps of the once-enslaved people, flooding into the city to find work. But Paramaribo, too, was riddled with poverty. They hoped for a chance to sit down at the little table in the back garden with the man who had returned from Holland with a fresh wind of resistance.

Cornelis Gerhard Anton de Kom was born in Paramaribo in 1898. He earned a degree in bookkeeping and worked for a while at the offices of the Balata Compagnie, which was in the business of harvesting balata, a kind of natural rubber. De Kom was struck by the difficult lives of the balata bleeders: laborers, mostly creoles (the term then in common use in Suriname for the descendants of freed slaves), who tapped the rubber trees in the stifling heat of the rainforest. He resigned and, in 1920, left for the Netherlands, where he married a Dutch woman, Petronella Borsboom.

As one of the few people of color in the country, De Kom came into contact with Javanese nationalists who were fighting for an independent Dutch East Indies: in other words, for Indonesia. That was when he first felt the winds of freedom blowing. He began to write articles for the Dutch Communist Party magazine; at the time, that was the only party with a clear anti-colonial stance. His articles and the revolutionary thrust of his arguments caught the attention of the Surinamese labor movement. He was especially popular with that group for criticizing wage reductions for indentured workers.

In late 1932, De Kom and his wife and children, four by then, returned to Suriname by ship to look after his ailing mother – who died during their voyage. Like-minded Surinamers were eagerly looking forward to De Kom's visit. In the backyard of his childhood home, he set up an advisory agency and took meticulous notes on his visitors' grievances. The Javanese, who felt disadvantaged relative to other ethnic groups, were the most likely to turn to "Papa De Kom," as they soon began to call him. Their heartfelt wish was that De Kom would lead them back to Java like a messiah. He wrote about them in *We Slaves of Suriname*: "Under the tree, past my table, files a parade of misery. Pariahs with deep, sunken cheeks. Starving people. People with no resistance to disease. Open books in which to read the story, haltingly told, of oppression and deprivation" (p. 203). De Kom promised to submit their grievances to the colonial authorities, but the unrest he caused was anything but welcome to Governor Abraham Rutgers.

On February 1, 1933, Anton de Kom led a group of supporters to the offices of the administration. He was arrested on suspicion of attempting to overthrow the regime.

From the street, none of the backyard is visible. The sidewall of the house is completely covered with zinc, and a large mango tree leans on the roof. In front of the neighboring house on that side, a woman is raking the fallen leaves and fruit into a pile. She is wearing a pink skirt, a tight sweater, a cap, and dark glasses. Like many people here, she probably bought her outfit from one of the cheap Chinese clothing shops found all over Paramaribo. The few with more to spend buy their clothes abroad or online. In some respects, today's city remains much like the Paramaribo in which De Kom grew up in the early twentieth century – even if the rich no longer live in the white-and-green mansions in the historic center, but in modern stone villas in leafy suburbs with names like Mon Plaisir and Elisabeths Hof.

It is not surprising that a revolutionary such as De Kom had his roots in a working-class district like Frimangron. In the days of slavery, enslaved people who had managed to purchase their freedom settled on the undeveloped outskirts of the city. Before then, emancipated house servants had made temporary homes in slave hovels in the backyards of Paramaribo's mansions. Frimangron literally means "freed people's land." On the long sand roads, the new citizens built simple dwellings and practiced trades. The main traffic artery was Pontewerfstraat. From its small workshops came the sounds of carpenters sawing and cobblers pounding and tapping, of tanners and tinsmiths. The women there did laundry or ironing for the white and light-skinned elite who held the power in the Dutch colony. This street, renamed after Anton de Kom in the early 1980s, is the location of the house where he was born.

De Kom must have spent a good deal of time as a child on the very stoop where the elderly man is now sitting. His father had been enslaved, and his grandmother taught her grandchildren about "the sufferings of slavery," in the words of De Kom's fierce indictment *We Slaves of Suriname*. He published the book in 1934, a year after the colonial authorities banished him from Suriname.

De Kom was a quick student and must have learned from a young age not to take injustice for granted. Many children in his neighborhood went barefoot, wore rags, and roamed the streets after dark. Education was compulsory, but few parents could afford the school fees, let alone decent shoes and school clothes. They had a hard enough time giving their children a simple meal, such as rice and salt fish, every day. If they could, they sent their children to work as kweekjes, sweeping, raking, and lugging pails of water for a wealthy family in return for room and board. Child labor was rife.

Anton de Kom's own childhood was probably easier. His father scraped together a living from his patch of soil and also worked as a gold miner. Young Anton must now and then have passed through Oranjeplein, a stately square in the alien realm of the city center, where the statue of Queen Wilhelmina stood in front of the governor's magnificent palace, although the monarch never visited her colony. Under the tamarind trees around the square, the upper middle class promenaded in their walking suits and long white dresses. In Frimangron, everyone was black. That is still mostly true today.

One Sunday morning, I drive down Anton Dragtenweg, along which handsome houses overlook the Suriname River. My destination is the district of Clevia: tight rows of Bruynzeel houses, mass-produced modular wooden dwellings with front and backyards. I park beside a recently sanded fence. "I'm painting the gate," Cees de Kom told me on the telephone, sounding a little breathless. Anton de Kom's son is now ninety-one years old but still looks sprightly. He invites me to walk up the stairs to the balcony ahead of him. His wife, one year younger, shakes my hand just as energetically.

Cees de Kom and I have something in common: we're both what used to be called "halfbloedjes," multiracial people with a black father and a white mother. The accepted term these days is "dubbelbloeden," not half but double bloods, and no longer in the childish diminutive form. When I speak to Cees at events – most recently at a screening of a film about his father's life – he never fails to point out this similarity between us. If anything in his life has left scars, it is being described as "half."

Cees, born in 1928, was four years old when the family arrived in Suriname. After his father's arrest, a crowd of protesters gathered in front of the administration offices to demand his release. The police opened fire. Two people were killed and twenty-two wounded. For more than three months, De Kom was held prisoner in Fort Zeelandia. By historical irony this was the very fort, built by the Dutch, where slaveholders could pay to have their so-called "disobedient slaves" disciplined. The Dutch colonists outdid both the English and the French in corporal and capital punishment; their methods included whipping, the cruel torture known as the "Spanish billy goat," the breaking wheel, and death by burning. De Kom's imprisonment must have added fuel to the fire of protest within him.

After he was exiled to the Netherlands, the intelligence service kept an eye on him. De Kom was seen as a communist, even though he never joined the Communist Party. He had tremendous difficulty finding work. "I remember my father was always writing," Cees tells me, "wearing his pencil down to a stub to save money. When World War II broke out, he joined the resistance and wrote for the illegal press. On August 7, 1944, he was arrested by the Germans. My mother sat looking out of the window for hours, hoping he would come back. But he never came. My brother and I were deported to Germany, where we worked on a farm.

"After we returned, we were told we had to leave again, this time to the Dutch East Indies. Restoring law and order there, that was our mission. And my father had sympathized with the Indonesian freedom fighters! I wrote a letter to the minister of defense asking for an exemption. My mother hadn't heard from my father since the liberation of the Netherlands. The most recent news we had was that he was being held in the German concentration camp Neuengamme. I didn't want to leave my mother until we found out what had happened to him, but that argument cut no ice with the Dutch authorities. Not until 1950 were we officially informed that my father had died in a camp on April 24, 1945." Cees points into the living room. "And my mother died in that chair right there – just gave up the ghost. We'd been living in Suriname for years by then, and she was visiting on vacation." A while ago, he decided the time had come to write his own memoirs: "All the dead weight you carry around." He hands me a thick manuscript in a ring binder. *Two Cultures, One Heart* is the title; underneath is a drawing of two overlapping circles, his parents' wedding rings.

"In the Netherlands, my name was written the usual Dutch way, with a K. I changed the spelling to Cees, which seemed more elegant to me, less Dutch, because in the Netherlands I could find no trace of my Surinamese culture."

As a boy, he was once on a tram with his father when a woman pointed out Anton to her child with a nod of the head and said, "Look, that's the bogeyman. Watch out, or he'll come and get you." There were also children who taunted Cees: "You don't have to buy soap, 'cause you'll always be dirty anyway." Later, still in the Netherlands, he worked for the PTT – the state postal, telegraph, and telephone service. One day he was discussing cultural differences with his co-workers, and a Dutch co-worker made the clumsy remark, "To people in Groningen I speak with an accent too, you know." On August 18, 1960, when his father's remains were reinterred in Loenen, the field of honor for those who died as a result of the war, all the names of the dead were read aloud except De Kom's. They were later told this had been a technical problem.

"One dirty trick after another," Cees says with a sigh. Always inferior, always misunderstood – he was sick and tired of it. Six years later, he and his family departed for his father's country on the ship *Oranje Nassau*. It was the same voyage his parents had made some thirty years earlier. But even in Suriname, as he discovered, the country's unique identity is often under-appreciated. "Almost all the books read here come from the Netherlands." The family, through a non-profit, owns the house where Anton de Kom was born, but they do not have the money to restore it. The government has neglected it altogether.

To throw off the yoke of Dutch rule – that was De Kom's aspiration when he wrote the book that has now become a classic: "No people can reach full maturity as long as it remains burdened with an inherited sense of inferiority. That is why this book endeavors to rouse the self-respect of the Surinamese people" (p. 85). In 2020, the forty-fifth anniversary of Surinamese independence, those words are as true as ever. In *We Slaves of Suriname*, De Kom was far ahead of his contemporaries – not only in Suriname, but also in the Netherlands. The land that the Netherlands had ruled for more than three hundred years would long remain a colonial blind spot. Only in the past few years has Suriname gained a modest place in Dutch collective awareness. This change is taking place in fits and starts, and the historical narrative coming into the spotlight is not always a pretty one.

When I was growing up in Amsterdam in the 1970s, I wrote a letter to the editors of my favorite girls' magazine, *Tina*. I was twelve years old. In my childish handwriting, I complimented them on their work and asked, "Why isn't there ever a colored girl on the cover?" Every day, I checked my mailbox for a reply. The fact that I never received one wounded me deeply.

Anton de Kom's work stands out both for its profound eloquence and for the courage with which he points out injustices. It is a tirade against the pragmatic spirit of commerce, the small shopkeeper's mindset that underlay the exploitation of a country and its people. Though its story is not by any means heartwarming, it *is* the story we share. The Dutch fathers of the colony boozed, fucked, and flogged with abandon, partly out of boredom and frustration with the tedium of plantation life. Such decadence would have been unthinkable in their own strait-laced homeland.

As a Surinamese schoolboy, De Kom had learned about Dutch sea rovers such as Piet Hein and Michiel de Ruyter and been required to memorize chronological lists of the colony's governors, the very men who had imported his African forefathers in the holds of slave ships. In his own book, he delves deep into the psyche of the slaveholders. He is hot on their trail, breathing down their necks, not letting up for a moment. You can practically see De Kom writing: perched on the edge of his chair, craning forward, pressing his stubby pencil to the paper. His style is supple, essayistic, and now and then lyrical, with unexpected imagery. Using the writer's toolkit, he infuses his work with color and emotion. And not once does he forget his own background, so aptly expressed by his use of an odo, a Surinamese proverb: the cockroach cannot stand up for its rights in the bird's beak.

When did the cover-up of this history really begin? For many years, anyone who brought it up could count on a patronizing response, something along the lines of "But look what the French or the British did, or the Africans themselves!" It's like the excuses made by buyers of stolen goods when caught red-handed. They point an insistent finger at the thief and the fence: it was *them*, not *me*! Yet without demand, there would be no supply. In a few places, monuments are being erected to commemorate the suffering, and explanatory labels are being placed next to statues of disgraced role models. But turning around and looking your own monster straight in the eyes still takes some effort.

We Slaves of Suriname still holds a mirror up to us today. The book delivers a message about might versus minority, capital versus poverty. Finding present-day parallels is easy enough; just look at the wretched circumstances of refugees in the Netherlands and other Western countries. Or Chinese shopkeepers working from early in the morning until late at night, in the clutches of a cartel. Or the drug rings in Latin America that extort money from ordinary citizens, or trafficking in women, or child labor in Asian textile factories. It is always systems that create the framework, and within them there are individuals who profit.

Oppression also depends crucially on stereotyping: us against the strange, unknown other. The rise of right-wing leaders around the world is, in large part, based on this us-and-them thinking. The Other is lazy or criminal, or both. "Do we want more or fewer Moroccans?" Dutch populist politician Geert Wilders has asked. Even firmer language was used in the Dutch campaign slogan "Act normal or go away."[1] "America First," but who does America really belong to? All these sound bites suggest a presumed right of ownership. De Kom was only too able to see through this type of spin. He followed the anonymous word "slaves" with the phrase "our fathers." Our fathers, not mere nameless creatures.

In the world after Anton de Kom, Mahatma Gandhi, Martin Luther King, Rosa Parks, Malcolm X, and Nelson Mandela, where are the human rights activists who will stand up to fight for rights that seem self-evident? Are the voices of opposition loud enough? Anton de Kom exposed the mechanisms of unfreedom. And of poverty. Therein lies the enduring power of his work.

On the sidewalk in front of Paramaribo's most famous hovel, the old man's flower is drooping in the heat. He stands and shuffles out into the street in his oversized slippers.

Note

1 Translator's note (TN): This 2017 slogan, a warning to immigrants, was part of a successful election campaign by the VVD, which presents itself as a mainstream right-wing libertarian party. After the March 2021 elections, the VVD remains the largest party in the parliament, with the large populist right-wing anti-immigrant PVV party led by Geert Wilders in third place.

The Breath of Freedom

We Slaves of Suriname as Literature

Duco van Oostrum

My work as a professor of American literature in England focuses on African-American writing. I am sometimes asked to say something about Dutch literature, and this led me to wonder: are there any well-known Black Dutch writers from the 1920s or 1930s? In the United States, that was the time of the Harlem Renaissance, the dawn of African-American literature, known for authors such as W.E.B. Du Bois, Langston Hughes, Nella Larsen, and Zora Neale Hurston. When I asked Dutch literary scholars if these writers had any counterparts in our country, the answer was, "Not that we know of."

An hour later, I was practically glued to my computer screen because, thanks to Google, I had found something. On the DBNL website, a digital database of Dutch-language literature, I had discovered *We Slaves of Suriname*, and I devoured it. Why hadn't I known about this book? De Kom combined the themes and style of Du Bois, the outrage of Frederick Douglass, the probing analyses of Langston Hughes, and Harriet Jacobs's struggle to share her story with the world. And all this in my own Dutch language, in a book about Suriname and about my country's own suppressed history of slavery.

My astonishment grew as I explored the analyses of *We Slaves*. I work in the academic context of literary theory with an emphasis on postcolonial and African-American theory, as formulated in classic studies by Henry Louis Gates (*The Signifying Monkey*, 1984), Paul Gilroy (*The Black Atlantic*, 1993), and Toni Morrison (*Playing in the Dark*, 1996). But *We Slaves* has consistently been brushed aside as a strange hodgepodge of history, sociology, and a pinch of autobiography, and faulted for De Kom's heavy reliance on earlier authors. *We Slaves of Suriname*, genuine literature? No, the scholars concluded, the term just didn't fit.

It reminds me of the words of Du Bois: "Between me and the other world there is ever an unasked question: unasked by some through feelings of delicacy; by others through the difficulty of rightly framing it. All, nevertheless, flutter round it ... How does it feel to be a problem?" (*Souls of Black Folk*, p. 9).

Yet by placing *We Slaves* in the context of African-American literature and theory, I intend to show that it is, in fact, a major work of Dutch literature. The "problem" of *We Slaves* as literature lies not in the book, nor in Anton de Kom, but in the prevailing perspectives on and framing of Dutch literature itself: what form it takes, who can write it, and how to read it.

Double Consciousness

We Slaves begins with a poetic ode to Suriname, interlaced with autobiography. This is directly followed by the historical narrative, from the beginnings of colonization to manumission (the release of enslaved people by their "owners") in 1863, the new wave of immigrants, and, lastly, De Kom's visit to and banishment from Suriname. It almost seems more like a collection of essays than a well-crafted story, and in a few places, De Kom directly addresses "the white reader," as if he knows some readers will respond to what they read with skepticism.

14

What are we to make of this blending of genres and the autobiographical approach? Note how De Kom links the history of slavery in Suriname to his own individual self: "the right to use and abuse one's living chattels, to buy and sell *our fathers and mothers*" (p. 54, italics DvO). This turns history into autobiography. In the African-American literary context, the form is practically traditional. Take, for example, W.E.B. Du Bois's *The Souls of Black Folk* (1903), which sheds light on African-American culture from many different angles – history, economics, anthropology, biography, fiction, autobiography, and cultural history – emphasizing each time how the alternative perspective can overturn received ideas. Du Bois underpins every one of his claims with detailed historical accounts and facts. Each chapter is rooted in his now-famous concept of *double consciousness*: "One ever feels his twoness, – an American, a Negro; two souls, two thoughts, two unreconciled strivings; two warring ideals in one dark body" (p. 11).

That same inner struggle, and the rewriting of the experience of double consciousness, come to the fore magnificently in *We Slaves*. Having grown up with the conventional Dutch history of Suriname as enshrined in the Winkler Prins encyclopedia, De Kom rewrote it by reinterpreting history and fictionalizing it from the perspective of the enslaved Black people. For example, he tells the story of Flora, Séry, and Séry's daughter Patienta, taken captive on a 1711 expedition. The child is torn from Séry's arms by "rough white hands." Séry trembles with fear but "no scream came from her lips; she simply gazed at Ensign Molinay with fire in her eyes and then rose to her feet, displaying her pride to the white soldiers, defying them all without the slightest fear" (p. 95). The story is told from the women's perspective, with Séry's gaze fixed on the eyes of the white colonizer, rather than from the point of view of the soldier. Then De Kom quotes a long passage from a classic work of history accepted by scholars as authoritative, J. Wolbers's *Geschiedenis van Suriname* ("History of Suriname," 1861), choosing to italicize some phrases, such as these from a report quoted by Wolbers:

> *Notwithstanding all the torments with fire and blows, we [Dutch soldiers] were never able to compel her to answer, for notwithstanding all this she remained as stubborn as ever, and by pointing at the sky, grasping a long lock of hair on her head, slapping her mouth with her fingers, and running her hand over her throat, she let us know she would rather have her head cut off than disclose any information, whether by speaking or by pointing the way.* (p. 96)

De Kom concludes that in this episode "defenseless Surinamese women fell into the hands of supposedly civilized Dutchmen who murdered them" and concludes with the words, "Brave Séry. Brave Flora. We will always commemorate and honor your names" (p. 97).

This rewriting and reversal of the narrative focus, shifting the center of attention from Molinay's failed expedition to the women's heroism, serves a crucial literary purpose. De Kom first situates us in Séry's perspective, looking through her fiery eyes, and then makes her central to a documentary historical narrative. Instead of being presented with stereotypes of enslaved Black people, we read about named individuals in old, historical Dutch.

In his manifesto of the Harlem Renaissance (*The New Negro*, 1925), Alain Locke writes that Black authors should portray an African-American as a fully fleshed literary character, and no longer as "more of a formula than a human being" (p. 3). He urges them to avoid stereotypes like those in Harriet Beecher Stowe's *Uncle Tom's Cabin* in favor of realistic characters that do not let themselves be defined by others but instead define themselves. That is exactly what De Kom does in this passage, presenting the women as the decision-makers, in control of the situation, even though they die.

De Kom employs another literary strategy also found in the work of Du Bois, using white history (such as Wolbers's work) as documented fact, as evidence for the truth of his own narrative. For example, De Kom keeps insisting that his book gives the "facts." He repeats this many times: "Once again, we would like to start by presenting a few facts by way of example" (p. 70). This is a rewriting of what is already in the archive.

Facts Forgotten and Facts Suppressed

And that cultural archive was bulging with material.[1] De Kom devotes one whole gruesome chapter to the "punishments" inflicted by the plantation owners, with details drawn from historical documents. In *We Slaves*, De Kom uses these documents to give literary form to facts forgotten and facts suppressed, so that the reader can no longer dismiss them as trivial.

Until the publication of *We Slaves*, much of the Dutch population felt that slavery in Suriname had been far away and irrelevant. They told themselves it couldn't have been as bad as all that. Yes, perhaps there had been a few unfortunate incidents – so the argument went – but that was a question of a few rotten apples spoiling the reputation of all plantation owners. Meanwhile, the investors in Surinamese plantations had often been banks or individuals in the Netherlands. African-American literature contests this "bad masters defense," often with horrifying facts and stories, and De Kom proceeds in exactly the same way, showing that the Dutch justice system had horrifying consequences. Because enslaved people were not seen as human beings but as possessions, public massacres came to be considered normal. The torture method known as the "Spanish billy goat" played a central role in all this; almost everyone has seen the prints by John Gabriel Stedman and William Blake. Surinamese slavery is known, despite continuing debate in some quarters in the Netherlands, as the cruelest form practiced by any Western power.

Another form of cruelty discussed by De Kom at length is the systematic sexual exploitation of "our mothers." They "worked" for their owners and produced still more Dutch chattels: the children they bore. His trenchant analysis shows that this practice was inspired not by any Christian ideology, but by the deep-seated Dutch love of the *koopje*, the cheap buy. To De Kom, the combination of putative Christianity and the desire for a cheap buy is unique to Surinamese slavery.

De Kom also rewrites the rainforest expeditions against the maroon leaders Joli Coeur, Baron, and Boni, describing them from those leaders' perspective and telling the stories of their individual backgrounds. He sets them in direct contrast to the governors heading the Dutch colonial administration and shows the reader that their conduct is more civilized than that of the "whites." He writes, "We defy one and all to show us that whites have ever, at any time in Surinamese history, treated colored people this way" (p. 115)! Role models like these, "our fathers and mothers," as De Kom consistently calls them, are the book's literary heroes.

> They were counted among the brutes, as the whites called the maroons in those days, but to us they are and will remain heroes of Suriname, who won their proud status as leaders through bravery and virtue, fighters for the rights and liberty of Surinamese slaves. Baron! Boni! Joli Coeur! Your memory will be forever cherished in our hearts. You are part of us. (p. 120)

Here De Kom places a literary image in the heart of the reader, so to speak – one which drives out any colonialist image of the maroon leaders. This revisioning from the perspective of the oppressed is central to the narration of the story of slavery. As Frederick Douglass reflected at the end of his life, "My part has been to tell the story of the slave. The story of the master has never wanted for narrators" (Douglass, pp. 310–311).

The Personal Decolonization of White Education

In the African-American literary tradition, we see similar depictions of heroes from the eighteenth century onwards. In 1853, Douglass wrote an essay about the heroic slave Madison Washington, and in *The Souls of Black Folk*, Du Bois grounded the Black thinker, teacher, and minister Alexander Crummell in the history of the American Reconstruction era. What such examples show is that the sense of inferiority stemming from enslavement, which De Kom discussed with the same sensitivity as Frantz Fanon, can be combatted through literary valorization. This amounts to the personal decolonization of white education. After his banishment, De Kom spent a great deal of time in the National Archives in The Hague and read the materials available to those outside the academic system.

Among African-American writers, the struggle to obtain information from outside the establishment was likewise crucial to the development of self-knowledge and self-confidence. To borrow books from the Chicago library, Richard Wright needed a note from a white sponsor. As he wrote in "The Ethics of Living Jim Crow," "I would write a note to the librarian, saying, 'Please let this n----- boy have the following books.' I would then sign it with the white man's name" (p. 14).

In prison, Malcolm X re-educated himself from the ground up by memorizing the dictionary. On the first page, he was struck by a word that comes from Afrikaans: "aardvark." And the young Frederick Douglass challenged other boys to write words down so that he could learn them.

The very act of writing undermines colonialist prejudices about the supposed unintelligence of enslaved people. Such prejudices formed the pretext for denying them formal education. In 1845, Frederick Douglass published his autobiography, *Narrative of the Life of Frederick Douglass, An American Slave*. This slave narrative immediately became a huge success, and part of its radicalism lay in its subtitle, *Written by Himself*.

By writing literature, an enslaved person defies one important tenet of the slavery system: enslaved people can never hold a position of any significance in white society and will always need support. Writings by enslaved people were dismissed as hoaxes, and critics argued that they had actually been written by white authors. Even De Kom, who published *We Slaves* almost ninety years after Douglass's book, met with this reaction. *We Slaves* was disregarded and belittled as "really written by Jeff Last." The implicit claim was that De Kom, a Black man, could not possibly possess the ability to write such a book. That argument was used to exclude him from Dutch culture.

Furthermore, De Kom's union activities and contributions to left-wing papers led to accusations of communism, and he thus came to be seen as a potential enemy of the Dutch state. In the United States, many African-American writers faced similar allegations in response to their political activities. The well-known gospel singer, actor, and activist Paul Robeson, for instance, was not permitted to renew his passport after the McCarthy hearings. Strikingly, De Kom's biography notes that he used to hum Robeson tunes (Woortman and Boots, p. 261). Du Bois emigrated to Ghana for idealistic reasons, and Richard Wright to France.

The Surinamese-Dutch American Otto Huiswoud, who moved from Suriname to Harlem during the Harlem Renaissance and became involved in political activism there, also left the United States. After World War II, he moved to the Netherlands, where his positions included the presidency of Vereniging Ons Suriname (the "Our Suriname Association"; V.O.S.).

The Breath of Freedom

That sense of inferiority can be counterbalanced by writing literature. De Kom states this in no uncertain terms: "No people can reach full maturity as long as it remains burdened with an inherited sense of inferiority. That is why this book endeavors to rouse the self-respect of the Surinamese people and also to demonstrate the falsehood ..." (pp. 85). This is also one reason for the autobiographical basis of many works in this Black literary tradition; as witness statements rooted in fact, the stories are necessarily true. The writers of the Harlem Renaissance built on the literary "I" developed in slave narratives like those of Frederick Douglass. The near-classic opening "I was born a slave" serves to show how the writer escaped that category and became an "I," a person with a human identity.

Langston Hughes wrote in "The Negro Artist and the Racial Mountain" (1926), "We younger Negro artists who create now intend to express our individual dark-skinned selves without fear or shame. ... We know we are beautiful. And ugly too." The authorship of "selves" is a central concern. That is why De Kom emphasizes the "We" in *We Slaves of Suriname*. Taking control of the literary presentation of "our own individual black-colored identity" is more or less the motto of *We Slaves*.

This understanding of "We" forms a fundamental departure from the "I" of much early African-American literature. De Kom thus emphasizes his conception of solidarity and the distortion of history. This is illustrated by two important passages from *We Slaves*.

When De Kom returned to Suriname in late December 1932 to visit his gravely ill mother, he stood on the deck of the ship longing for "Sranan, my fatherland," as he put it, amid the flying fish and "the breath of freedom." It is no stretch to see this as an allusion to the slave ships and the captivity associated with them. For example, in the best known of the rare literary accounts of the "Middle Passage" (from Africa to the Americas), *The Interesting Narrative of the Life of Olaudah Equiano or Gustavas Vassa, the African* (1789), the enslaved Olaudah Equiano described the flying fish on the deck and the contrast between the fresh air there and the stench in the hold. De Kom goes on to describe his encounter with a white stoker:

> High in the stays and shrouds of the Rensselaer blows the wind of freedom. On the deck below me, a stoker emerges – white, but blacker than I am with soot from his fire – and hurries toward his stuffy quarters. Halfway along the forecastle, he waves at me and the children. In the blackness of his face, the whites of his eyes and his pearly teeth are smiling. That too is the same everywhere, and beautiful everywhere: the fellowship among proletarians and their love of liberty. (p. 200)

The stoker and De Kom embody a new "we," "the same everywhere, and beautiful everywhere," which champions the love of liberty. In this passage, we witness an unexpected encounter between white and Black: not a sense of alienation from one another, but a look of recognition, a laugh, and a wave. De Kom recognizes the stoker and himself as equals, in spite of all their differences.

These passages in *We Slaves* deserve literary analysis to uncover new textual meanings. In reading his final chapter purely as autobiography, the reader overlooks De Kom's added nuances and creative choices.

A Vision of Motherly Listening
Here, in closing, is another key passage from the final chapter of *We Slaves*. In it, De Kom lays out his literary

vision, in much the same way as Du Bois in *The Souls of Black Folk*. While Du Bois sees the sorrow songs and African-American music as the instruments of positive change in American culture, De Kom describes his vision through the story of his arrival in Suriname, where he is hailed as a savior. At that stage, he doesn't quite know what to do; he is under surveillance by investigators and forbidden to give speeches.

> It's as though someone has suddenly knocked at my heart: What will you do to ease your people's suffering? In the velvet darkness of the night I hear soft steps.
>
> Mother, what can I do to help? My comrades are waiting. I have only just returned. So much has changed.
>
> It seems as if my mother leans in to kiss me, the way she did when I was little, the way she listened to my complaints and my sorrow ebbed away because someone was willing to listen.
>
> And all at once I know: I will open an advisory agency and listen to the complaints of my fellows, the same way my mother once listened to her son's sorrows. (p. 202)

De Kom had traveled to Suriname with his wife and children to see and speak to his mother, but she died not long before his arrival. It is as if that personal trauma of arriving too late is transformed into this image, this vision of motherly listening as the driving force of change. Not the archetypal male response of fighting back, as Frederick Douglass fought the "Negro-breaker" Covey, but listening and working with others: that is the vision that comes to De Kom in *We Slaves*.

It is striking that this key passage has gone almost unnoticed in discussions and interpretations of *We Slaves*, with the emphasis placed instead on the autobiographical person and on communist allegations about a kind of revolution. In *We Slaves*, this revolutionary vision is explicitly rejected. Ndyukas, members of a maroon people, want to conceal weapons on the grounds of De Kom's house. But De Kom writes:

> Almost every day, representatives of the Ndyukas of Boven-Commewijne came to me, and I received a number of offers to bring weapons to my property in secret, offers I rejected in the most forceful terms. What I was after was organization, not a bloodbath. (p. 208)

Instead of promoting violent resistance, De Kom tries to achieve change through a strategy of listening. His mother listened to his complaints, and that helped "because someone was willing to listen." De Kom listens to the complaints of "his fellows," and today's reader listens to De Kom.

In Suriname, De Kom was taken prisoner and confined to Fort Zeelandia. Here too, there is a parallel to many African-American writers such as Douglass, Jacobs, and Malcolm X, who all spent time in American prisons in the course of their lives and wrote about their experiences.

I hope it is clear by now that De Kom's experiences, his journey toward self-knowledge and self-confidence, and his writing stand in a literary context and tradition. One significant contrast with the African-American context, however, is that many North American college students are assigned Frederick Douglass or W.E.B. Du Bois as required reading in a survey of American literature. My son, who is studying at an American university, recently asked me if I would read his essay about Douglass. African-American works have entered the canon of American literature, and there are now essays comparing "Call me Ishmael" (the famous opening sentence of Herman Melville's *Moby-Dick*) to "I was born a slave." Like Melville, Douglass is now seen as an American cultural icon.

The same cannot yet be said of De Kom in the Netherlands. I read Simon Vestdijk's *Back to Ina Damman* (1934) in secondary school in the Netherlands many years ago, as a text exemplifying Dutch literature and culture of the 1930s. Perhaps now, students will read *We Slaves* alongside the canonical Vestdijk, analyze these texts together, and establish a different, inclusive Dutch literary canon of the early twentieth century. Maybe then a new Dutch literary "We" of interconnection will emerge, a "We" of listening and sharing.

Note

1 In her book *White Innocence* (2016), Gloria Wekker uses the term "cultural archive" to reinvestigate perspectives on Dutch culture. [DvO]

Bibliography

Douglass, Frederick. *Narrative of the Life of Frederick Douglass, An American Slave, Written by Himself.* London: W.W. Norton, 2016 (1845).

Douglass, Frederick. 'From *The Life and Times of Frederick Douglass* (1892)'. In *The Oxford Frederick Douglass Reader.* Ed. William L. Andrews. Oxford: Oxford University Press, 1996, pp. 226–311.

Du Bois, W.E.B. *The Souls of Black Folk.* London: W.W. Norton, 1999 (1903). The 1903 edition was published under his full, partly Dutch, name: W.E. Burghardt Du Bois.

Equiano, Olaudah. *The Interesting Narrative and Other Writings.* Ed. Vincent Carretta. London: Penguin, 1995 (1789).

Gates, Henry Louis. *The Signifying Monkey: A Theory of African-American Literary Criticism.* Oxford: Oxford University Press, 1988.

Gilroy, Paul. *The Black Atlantic: Modernity and Double-Consciousness*. London: Verso, 1993.

Hughes, Langston. "The Negro Artist and the Racial Mountain." *The Nation*, June 23, 1926. Online: https://www.thenation. com/issue/june-23-1926/

Jacobs, Harriet. *Incidents in the Life of a Slave Girl: Written by Herself*. Ed. L. Maria Child. London: Harvard University Press, 1987 (1861).

Kom, Anton de. *Wij slaven van Suriname*. Amsterdam: Atlas Contact, 2017 (1934).

Locke, Alain. *The New Negro: Voices of the Harlem Renaissance*. New York: Simon and Schuster, 1999 (1925).

Morrison, Toni. *Playing in the Dark: Whiteness and the Literary Imagination*. London: Harvard University Press, 1992.

Stedman, John Gabriel. *Narrative of a Five Years Expedition against the Revolted Negroes of Surinam*. Eds. Richard Price and Sally Price. London: Johns Hopkins University Press, 1988 (1790/1796).

Stowe, Harriet Beecher. *Uncle Tom's Cabin*. London: W.W. Norton, 1994 (1852).

Vestdijk, Simon. *Terug tot Ina Damman*. Amsterdam: Nijgh & Van Ditmar, 1999 (1934).

Wekker, Gloria. *White Innocence: Paradoxes of Colonialism and Race*. London: Duke University Press, 2016.

Wolbers, Julien. *Geschiedenis van Suriname*. London: British Library, Historical Print Editions, 2011 (1861).

Woortman, Rob and Alice Boots. *Anton de Kom. Biografie, 1898–1945 | 1945–2009*. Amsterdam: Atlas Contact, 2009.

Wright, Richard. "The Ethics of Living Jim Crow: An Autobiographical Sketch." In *Uncle Tom's Children*. New York: Harper & Row, 1993 (1938), pp. 3–15. Library book episode at p. 14.

X, Malcolm with Alex Haley. *The Autobiography of Malcolm X*. London: Penguin, 2001 (1965).

Why Anton de Kom Still Inspires Generation after Generation

Mitchell Esajas

It is an honor to write an essay about one of my heroes, Anton de Kom. I can't remember when I first read his book, but I do know that my mother, who was born into a large farm family in Coronie, Suriname, had a beautiful edition of *We Slaves of Suriname* on the shelf. On the cover was a portrait of De Kom and above that the title in bold pink and orange letters.

As I write, in 2020, the latest Dutch edition is soon to be published. On the one hand, this is a praiseworthy decision on the publisher's part, eighty-six years after the first edition. On the other hand, it is sad to think that one reason the book has been reissued is its contemporary significance. In *We Slaves of Suriname*, De Kom showed in a compelling, probing, and illuminating way that, even after the abolition of slavery, colonialism perpetuated inequality. Many things have changed, but unfortunately we are still, even now in 2020, grappling with the legacy of colonialism. Many generations have drawn strength and inspiration from De Kom's work. This essay – which is based on documents from The Black Archives, a center for the documentation of Surinamese, Caribbean, and African history – aims to show how Anton de Kom has inspired different generations.

"Race" and Class in Colonial Surinamese Society

One of the reasons De Kom's work inspires so many people is that he was the first Surinamese writer to make a razor-sharp analysis of how racism and class functioned in Surinamese colonial society. Even after July 1, 1863, formerly enslaved people, along with indentured workers who had recently arrived in the country, were still doing the demanding physical labor for the benefit of the white colonial elite and large companies. De Kom saw discrimination against indentured workers from what were then the Dutch East Indies and British India and in favor of European immigrants. He also made it clear that employers were exploiting indentured workers by persuading them, "under false pretenses, to sign contracts that keep wages low and working conditions poor in Suriname and perpetuate the old slave mentality" (p. 163).

He also provided his readers with a visceral understanding of the wretched and inhumane circumstances under which the indentured workers and formerly enslaved people were practically forced to work for meager wages on coffee and sugar plantations and as "balata bleeders" deep in the Surinamese rainforest. De Kom describes how the treatment of Black and brown laborers contrasted with that of a group of white German laborers who settled in the colony in 1897. The difference is shocking: many of the Black and brown indentured workers did not survive the voyage to Suriname, because of "malnourishment, a lack of fresh air, and filthy berths" (p. 163).

Solidarity

De Kom did not, however, hold all white people responsible for the suffering and exploitation of the Surinamese people. On the contrary, during his years in the Netherlands he was in communication with socialists, communists, and nationalists from various backgrounds, including some from what is now Indonesia. This made him aware of the intersection between racism and the economic system. In his book, De Kom addressed white Dutch workers directly:

> We ask the Dutch workers: slavery has been abolished in Suriname, but can you call those who are forced to work under such a contract truly free? (p. 152)

De Kom saw white workers not as enemies or as competitors but as potential comrades in the struggle for all people to live in dignity. He must have learned from communist periodicals such as *Links richten* ("Aim Left") about the international labor movements that were at their height in the 1930s.

In 1934, Anton met another Surinamese resistance fighter, Otto Huiswoud. Like De Kom, Huiswoud had been born after the abolition of slavery, and in the early twentieth century he had made his way to New York. In 1919, he became the only Black co-founder of the Communist Party of the United States of America. He and his wife Hermina Dumont-Huiswoud traveled the world in support of their ideal: a global revolution through class struggle.

What did De Kom and Otto Huiswoud talk about? The archives show that, along with the artist Nola Hatterman, they attended an Anti-Imperialist League conference in Paris together. The Huiswouds were the editors of the communist newspaper *The Negro Worker*; in the June 1934 edition, they published an English-language article by De Kom entitled "Starvation, hunger and misery in Dutch Guyana." In that international forum, De Kom sharply criticized Suriname's colonial system, writing:

> We remember the 16 million florins, Holland gave the white slave barons as indemnity for the emancipated slaves. These millions were given to the Bakras (whites) as a reward for the inhuman deeds they committed against the

Negro slaves our forefathers. But to the slaves and today to the free Negroes not a penny. Their only reward today is unemployment, misery and starvation.

Only through organization and struggle can the workers of Dutch Guiana succeed in bettering their living conditions and effectively fight against the exploitation and slavery imposed upon them by the Dutch colonial rulers.

Only through solidarity and joint struggle between the workers of the capitalist countries and the colonial toilers can an effective blow be dealt to the common enemy: Imperialism. Workers, organize and fight against exploitation, unemployment, and starvation! Close ranks in struggle for the emancipation of the colonial toilers!

Demand the independence of Dutch Guiana!

This relatively brief article was written in a style very similar to that of *We Slaves of Suriname*: clear examples of the exploitation of Surinamese workers, a comparison to exploitation in the days of slavery, and an appeal to workers to unite. The striking thing is that in this article he explicitly called for Surinamese independence. De Kom often wrote about "workers" and "proletarians." His objective was to unite workers from diverse backgrounds:

> And maybe I will find a way to make them feel some fraction of the hope and courage contained in that one powerful word I learned in a foreign country: organization. Maybe I can put an end to some of the dissension that has been the weakness of these colored people; maybe it will not prove completely impossible to make Negroes, Hindustanis, Javanese, and Indians understand that only solidarity can unite all the sons of Mother Sranan in their struggle to live with dignity. (p. 202)

This razor-sharp analysis and message of struggle, sometimes presented in a poetic, literary manner, and sometimes in a factual, historical way, is what still inspires generation after generation. De Kom's insights into the decades-long impact of the legacy of slavery and the colonial system, both in Suriname and in the Netherlands, give the book its timeless relevance. When we talk about Black history, our thoughts often leap to the Black intellectuals and freedom fighters who left us their timeless work, to figures such as Martin Luther King Jr., Marcus Garvey, Angela Davis, Malcolm X, and Frantz Fanon. Anton de Kom's words and deeds have earned him a place among them.

A New Generation Rediscovers Anton de Kom

We Slaves of Suriname was published in 1934, but it was made difficult to obtain for a long time, even after the war. How did this change? According to former members of the Surinaamse Studenten Unie ("Surinamese Student Union"; SSU), one important step was the discovery of a copy of the book by the Surinamese student Rubia Züschen in the Leiden University Library in the 1960s. Züschen was a member of the SSU, which was known for being a hotbed of politically engaged left-wing students who supported the decolonization of Suriname. These students were so inspired by the book that they decided to retype the entire manuscript and distribute clandestine copies. Delano Veira was a member of the Vereniging Ons Suriname and in frequent communication with the SSU. In a conversation about his memories of Anton de Kom, he said:

> Anton de Kom was the shining example for Surinamese students in the Netherlands in the 1950s and 60s, because he was the first to hold Surinamese colonialism up to the light in such a fiery way. And he lived up to his words; he returned to Suriname himself, and we all know about that historic episode: two or more people were shot dead by the colonial regime in the uprisings, and Anton de Kom was banished.[1]

The 1970s saw a rise in anti-colonial consciousness among the Surinamese in the Netherlands and in Suriname, partly under the influence of the international decolonization struggle in former colonies in Africa and Asia. In 1972, the Vereniging Ons Suriname established a non-profit organization for community welfare called Bouw Een Surinaamse Tehuis ("Build A Surinamese Center," B.E.S.T.). They occupied a vacant building in the Amsterdam city center and declared it the Centrum Anton de Kom ("Anton de Kom Center"), a social and cultural center for Surinamese people in the Netherlands. The monthly magazine *Adek*, short for Anton de Kom, reported on injustices with which Surinamese people were confronted in the Netherlands, such as racism, discrimination, and police brutality. It also dealt with problems in Suriname, such as poor government policies and unemployment.

In 1973 Vereniging Ons Suriname, in cooperation with other organizations such as the Amsterdam student unions SRVU and ASVA, organized an "Anton de Kom month" to mark the fortieth anniversary of the uprising after De Kom's arrest. This month of talks and discussions focused on Anton de Kom and his ideas.

Fifteen years later, in June 1988, an event commemorating Anton de Kom was organized by the Anton de Kom–Abraham Behr-instituut, a collective founded by Surinamese activists from the Landelijke Strijd Organisatie voor Surinamers ("National Activist Organization for the Surinamese," LOSON) in partnership with the V.O.S. A number of people who had known De Kom personally in the World War II resistance spoke of him in glowing terms. His daughter Judith de Kom, an anti-colonial activist in her own right, also participated in the event.

Memories of the man whose work has such profound meaning to the Surinamese people and is also unquestionably part of the rich activist tradition of the Dutch

1933 FEBRUARI 1973

ANTON DE KOM-MAAND

Monthly magazine *Adek* © The Black Archives

labor movement. Memories that complete and bring to life the image of De Kom as a great humanist, as a revolutionary activist against exploitation and oppression, as an internationalist. Full of humanity and full of fight.[2]

Bram Behr, who was assassinated in Suriname's December murders of 1982 after criticizing the country's military dictatorship, wrote to his friends that reading *We Slaves of Suriname* had given him courage. Around the same time,

From left to right, Armand Baag, Zapata Jaw, Ronald Snijders,
and Judith de Kom performing at Vereniging Ons Suriname
in the 1970s, with a portrait of Anton de Kom on the wall
© The Black Archives

LOSON circulated a petition demanding the rehabilitation
of Anton de Kom. This resulted in the renaming of a
square after De Kom in Amsterdam's Zuidoost (Southeast)
district, near the present location of the Bullewijk metro
stop. Today, the central market square where the district's
municipal offices are located bears De Kom's name, and a
statue of De Kom towers over the square.

In the Surinamese community, De Kom is a hero and
part of our collective consciousness. But outside it, he is
still sadly unknown to many people.

The Legacy of Slavery
Anton de Kom is also a hero to today's activists. This
became clear when a group of Surinamese, African,
and Caribbean Dutch people spoke out in protest in

Amsterdam's Oosterpark on July 1, 2014 – the day of Keti Koti, the annual celebration of emancipation in Suriname. Before Lodewijk Asscher, then deputy prime minister and social affairs minister, was scheduled to speak, the protesters made the following statement:

> We stand here today with the greatest possible respect and reverence for our ancestors. We stand here for Anton, Boni, Tula, Baron, Sophie, Joli Coeur, Tata, Karpata, Toussaint, Nanny, and the countless invisible fighters and victims of Dutch wealth and prosperity. We are here to make sure that no foreign breath will intrude on their commemoration. Minister Lodewijk Asscher represents the Dutch government, the same government that treats the Black community with disrespect, opposes a national day of commemoration, flouts UN conventions, and could not care less about the pain and the concerns of the Black community.

Furthermore, a beautiful statue of De Kom made by the artist Edwin de Vries was included in the Great Suriname Exhibition in De Nieuwe Kerk in Amsterdam, which ran from late 2019 to early 2020. Around the same time, my mother's copy of *We Slaves of Suriname* was on display in the exhibition "Afterlives of Slavery" in Amsterdam's Tropenmuseum.

Although slavery in Suriname was abolished on paper 157 years ago, in 1863, its legacy is still seen and felt by many people in the form of everyday racism, institutional racism, and structural inequality in diverse segments of society. In education, Black children are confronted with discrimination by fellow students and by teachers, as well as with a lopsided curriculum in which the sinister sides of the colonial past are usually hushed up.[3] Numerous studies have shown that job applicants with a migrant background are less likely to find work than white applicants, because of their skin color, name, or cultural background.

Recent years have seen a growing movement opposing institutional racism in the Netherlands. An all-time low was reached in November 2019, when a conference organized by the activist group Kick Out Zwarte Piet, which opposes the blackface character Zwarte Piet involved in celebrations of Sinterklaas (St. Nicholas's Eve) in the Dutch-speaking world, was violently disrupted by radicalized pro-Zwarte Piet protesters. This shows that, in a different era and in a different way, it remains essential for us to continue Anton de Kom's struggle.

De Kom understood that education is an essential means of achieving justice and equality:

> No better way to foster a sense of inferiority in a race than through this form of historical education, in which the sons of a different people are the only ones mentioned or praised. It took a long time before I could free myself entirely from the obsessive belief that a Negro is always and unreservedly inferior to any white. (p. 84)

Today, in 2020, we might turn this message around. I believe that most Surinamese people have already thrown off the colonial sense of inferiority to white people. Yet there are still white people who, perhaps unconsciously, harbor a sense of superiority. It expresses itself in part in the ferocity and aggressiveness with which they defend the Sinterklaas tradition, which symbolizes the colonial power structures De Kom opposed. But we also see it in the institutional racism that still affects many Black people and people of color. Anton de Kom's struggle is unfortunately not over yet, but his work and his ideas continue to inspire new generations. I myself find new insights in *We Slaves of Suriname* with every read, and it reminds me that the work I do with my colleagues at The Black Archives and in the anti-racism movement builds on the work of giants such as Anton de Kom.

Notes

1 From the mini-documentary *Vereniging Ons Suriname: 100 jaar emancipatie & strijd*: https://www.youtube.com/watch?v=wHJVOcBVzw0. [ME]
2 *A. de Kom, zijn strijd en ideeën*. Edited by the Anton de Kom–Abraham Behr Institute. Sranan Buku, Amsterdam 1989. [ME]
3 http://www.republiekallochtonie.nl/blog/achtergronden/racisme-en-discriminatie-treffen-surinaamse-nederlanders-op-de-arbeidsmarkt. [ME]

Foreword

Judith de Kom

TRUTH raises itself against the storm that scatters its seeds broadcast.

Rabindranath Tagore

"No people can reach full maturity as long as it remains burdened with an inherited sense of inferiority. That is why this book endeavors to rouse the self-respect of the Surinamese people." These are the words of Anton de Kom in the section "The History of Our Nation" (p. 85).

He foresaw that the Surinamese people, weighed down by the legacy of colonialism, would have to walk a long, hard road to develop into a full-fledged nation.

We Slaves of Suriname is partly a political commentary on the history of Suriname and partly a cry for justice. Most importantly, perhaps, it was written by a child of Suriname whose dissenting opinions brought the force of colonial oppression down upon him.

Anton de Kom was born in Paramaribo in 1898.

"He was a quiet child. As a boy, he was always lost in a book," family members say.

His father was a gold-digger. After the gold industry went into decline, he took up farming. There were six children in the family, three boys and three girls. Anton

39

was the eldest son. He went to the Paulusschool in Paramaribo, going on after primary school to "advanced elementary education," an unusual step for a child from his background in 1910.

Letters of reference indicate that he then became an office worker. His employers included H.C. Cooke, a process server and debt collector; he also spent three years at the Balata Compagnieën Suriname en Guyana.

This last position brought him in touch with the balata bleeders (harvesters of natural rubber). It became his first struggle against exploitation. A worker who knew him said, "He sat in his office and fought for us. He made sure we received the wages to which we were entitled."

In June 1920, De Kom left for the Netherlands, where he volunteered for the 2nd Cavalry Regiment. After serving for one year, he left the military and found work as an assistant accountant. In January 1926, De Kom married Petronella C. Borsboom. They would have three boys and one girl.

In the 1920s, as one of the few people of color in the Netherlands, he came into contact with the Indonesian nationalist students, such as Mohammed Hatta, who would later play such an important role in the political awakening and liberation of Indonesia. It was partly thanks to them that De Kom's political consciousness was raised. Another contributing factor was Black activism in the Americas, the work of Marcus Garvey among others. He met left-wing Dutch writers and became a good public speaker, giving lectures on his country, Suriname, and against colonialism.

"A socially engaged man, quiet and modest, but fierce in his response to injustice and exploitation," say those who knew him.

In December 1932, De Kom returned to his homeland for family reasons. The social situation there was disgraceful. Nothing had changed since 1920: the same high child mortality rate, the same malnourishment, the same unemployment, the same slums, the same poor health care. De Kom decided to found a consulting agency. He listened to the complaints of the people and urged solidarity and organization. All this was seen by the colonial authorities as a threat. They intervened and arrested De Kom.

On February 7, 1933, hundreds of Afro-, Indo-, and Javanese Surinamese went to the colony's chief public prosecutor to demand the release of the man who had stood up for their rights. The police unexpectedly opened fire on the crowd. Two people were killed and a number of others were wounded.

After three months' imprisonment without trial, De Kom was put on a ship to the Netherlands in May 1933. His expulsion, his political activities, and the Great Depression made life far from easy for him and his family in the Netherlands.

In World War II, he opposed fascism with vigor. Because of his writings for the underground press, he was arrested by the Germans in August 1944 and deported to a concentration camp in Germany, where he died in April 1945. Others interned there later described the courage with which De Kom had borne the humiliations of his captivity and recalled how often he spoke of his beloved Suriname.

The value system by which he lived – the unhesitating rejection of poverty, oppression, and exploitation – can still be found in his book *We Slaves of Suriname*.

The story of his life, despite its tragedy, holds a message of optimism and hope. For a short time, De Kom was able to unite his homeland's diverse ethnic groups in a struggle for life with dignity!

May this bring the Surinamese lasting hope and inspiration.

On behalf of the De Kom family
March 1981

We Slaves of Suriname

"Sranan," Our Fatherland

From 2 to 6 degrees south latitude, from 54 to 58 degrees west longitude, spanning from the blue of the Atlantic to the inaccessible Tumuc-Humac Mountains, which form the watershed with the Amazon Basin, between the broad expanses of the Corentyne and Maroni Rivers, which separate us from British and French Guiana, rich in immense forests, where the greenheart, the barklaki, the kankantri, and the prized brownheart grow, rich in wide rivers, where the heron, ibis, flamingo, and wiswisi nest, rich in natural treasures, in gold and bauxite, in rubber, sugar, plantains, and coffee ... poor in humankind, poorer still in human kindness ...[1]

> Sranan – our fatherland.
> Suriname, as the Dutch call it.
> Their country's twelfth and richest, no, their country's
>   poorest province.

Between the coast and the mountains our mother, Sranan, has slumbered for a thousand years and a thousand more. Nothing has changed in the dense forests of her unknown interior.

The primeval forests of the uplands seem sunk in a centuries-old silence, coming alive only at nightfall with the murmuring hum, like secret music, of thousands of insects. More romantic, but also more savage, is the landscape of the savannahs and along the rivers. Winding curtains of vine hang from the trees and block the way; wild orchids bloom; here skittish pakiras make their home, capuchin monkeys balance on branches, parrots let out their shrill cries, the jaguar lurks, and an armadillo probes for ants with its pointed tongue.

For thousands of years, the dark forests of Mother Sranan have been waiting, untouched and undeveloped. They harbor strange creatures whose names are hardly known in the West:[2] tree-dwelling tamanduas and prehensile-tailed porcupines, vireos and tanagers, the tigriman and the blauwdas, golden-collared toucanets on the high tops of the palms, and swarms of butterflies: the magnificent blue morphos and the yellow and orange cloudless sulphurs, often rising to just below the crowns of the trees.

People?

People are scarcely present to enjoy this beauty.

In the lowland live the Waraos, the Arawaks, and the Caribs, Indian tribes now weak and dying out, powerless descendants of the indigenous peoples who were expelled from the best places by the whites. In the highland, the Trios and the Wayanas. Their beadwork, artful braiding, and delicate ornaments for dancing all express their innate sense of beauty.

There are around 2,450 Indians in all, and some 17,000 maroons – Negroes living in the forests, of whom we will speak later.

No more than twenty thousand people inhabit Sranan's interior, an area almost five times the size of the Netherlands. Beyond that, the forests are peopled solely by sloths and agoutis, by spider monkeys, tapirs, and capybaras, by the howler monkey, the anteater, and the aboma sneki.

History has passed Mother Sranan by; three centuries of Dutch colonization have left her interior untouched. Her rapids power no engines; her fertile land is unsown, the rich treasures of her forests unexploited; in abject poverty, in shabby ignorance, the wild tribes live amid a natural bounty that goes to pointless waste.

Whites rarely venture into these wildernesses, where only the Indians and the maroons know the way. Along the river courses, a discharged French soldier, a British rowdy, or a Dutch naturalist sometimes penetrates the landscape. He plunges his knife into the white skin of the balata tree, releasing its precious, milky sap. But the former soldier returns to the coast, the rowdy drinks himself to death in a whisky haze by his lonesome campfire, the Dutchman is taken back downriver by maroons in a canoe; the wilderness is left behind, the wounds in the rubber trees scar over, and the deserted camp is overgrown with creepers.

Of Dutch influence, Dutch energy, and Dutch civilization there is not a trace in the Surinamese interior: not a road, not a bridge, not a house in which Dutch history is inscribed. The whites felt nothing but fear in the face of that wilderness, where their escaped slaves sought refuge. A pathetic, neglected railway, which goes nowhere and was never completed, is the sole remnant of a brief fever dream of gold.

The wide plains of the savannahs, the forests, and the tall granite mountains of Mother Sranan have been sleeping for hundreds of centuries.

For them no history has yet been written.

Only on the thin ribbon along the coast, here and there at the mouths of the big rivers, on the most fertile of the alluvial grounds, does the red, white, and blue of the Dutch tricolor wave.

Red –

"Look, Mother," the little white boy says in astonishment in Magdeleine Paz's wonderful book *Frère noir* ("Black Brother"), "you see? The Negroes have red blood too!"

White –

The color of Crommelin's peace treaties.

And blue?

Is it the color of our tropical sky, at which we gaze up through the dark leaves of our trees, to read in the twinkling stars the promise of a new life?

No, it is the deep blue of the Atlantic Ocean, across which the slave ships carried their African prizes, their living merchandise, our parents and grandparents, to their new fatherland Sranan.

The Era of Slavery

The Arrival of the Whites

> The ancient people who, to their own ruin, showed hospitality to the wealth-crazed crew of a Spanish caravel and to a man named "bearer of Christ." A people hounded ...
>
> Albert Helman[1]

In the words of a French author, "Fortunate the nation that knows no history."

The history of Suriname dates back to the discovery of the Wild Coast (the Guianas) by the whites in 1499.

We know from Hartsinck how the Wild Coast looked in those days.[2] It was home to an Indian people who were lord and master of their realm. "Being hospitable," Wolbers writes in his history of Suriname, "they often received visits from other members of their tribe, during which the conversation tended to revolve around the cherished topics of hunting and fishing. They possessed a certain inborn honesty and righteousness that shone through all their actions; they even displayed a courtesy and friendliness that one would not expect of uncivilized peoples. When they conversed with each other, their tone was always calm and gentle; they never spoke scornful words to one another. They also had some understanding

49

of the motion of the stars, which was very useful to them for finding their way in the wilderness."[3]

This description remains consistent with what explorers tell us today about the character of their descendants, the Trios and the Wayanas. They too are calm and gentle people, among whom intense emotional outpourings and uproarious laughter are rarely observed; they too are renowned for their warm generosity, their courage, and their enterprising spirit; they too are excellent boat pilots with expert knowledge of the rainforest. And yet they are nothing but vestiges, stunted in their natural development, of what was once an independent and happy people.

What drove the whites to these "wild" coasts? What sense of mission possessed them? What tidings, what happiness, what civilization did they have to offer this free and happy people? Did they, the first Spaniards who visited our shores, come to bring Guyana the blessings of the auto-da-fé and the Inquisition? Did they bring the same toleration, in the name of Christ, that Spain was then showing to Jews and Moors, or the white civilization of the breaking wheel, death by burning, and other tortures? Was that the legal basis for their invasion? Or was their sole reason for coming, with their red and yellow flags flying, to bring the message that gold is always bought with blood?

We will allow the facts to answer.

In 1492, Columbus discovered America, and soon the exaggerated accounts of the new land and its riches exerted an irresistible pull on Europeans of every class and rank.

Professor Werner Sombart has written about them in *Der Bourgeois*:[4]

> One species of the business [of sea-robbery] was the voyages of discovery which had become so numerous

since the fifteenth century. It is true that in the majority of cases all sorts of non-material motives were responsible for the enterprises – science, religion, glory, or pure adventure; yet the strongest, and often enough the only moving influence was the desire for gain. In reality these voyages were nothing more than well-organized raiding expeditions to plunder lands beyond the sea; more especially after the reports of Columbus, that on his voyages of discovery he had come across veritable gold-dust.[5] El Dorado henceforth became the avowed or implied goal of all the expeditions. Digging for treasure and gold-making, these superstitions were now united to a third – the search for a new land where gold could be gathered by the spadeful.

What manner of men led these expeditions? They were strong, healthy adventurers, sure of victory, brutal and greedy, conquering all before them. Common as they were in those days, they have more and more ceased to exist in our own. These attractive, ruthless sea-dogs, who abounded more especially in England in the sixteenth century, were made of the same stuff as the leaders of hired bands in Italy of the type of Francesco Sforza and Caesar Borgia, only they were more intent on the acquisition of gold and goods. They were thus more akin to the capitalist undertaker than their Italian predecessors.

[...]

It may be asked, what is my reason for bringing these conquerors and robbers into connection with capitalism? The answer is simple enough. Not so much because they themselves were a sort of capitalist undertaker, but principally because the spirit within them was identical with that in all trade and colony planting right down to the middle of the eighteenth century. The two were equally expeditions of adventure and conquest. Adventurer, Sea-robber, and Merchant are but three imperceptible stages in development.

El Dorado

El Dorado.
The Land of Gold.
Even now, the name has lost none of its wondrous power.

Even now, on the big passenger ship, a young doctor steps out into the night, his eyes dazzled by the lights of the ballroom, his thoughts swaying to the tipsy rhythms of the jazz band, and it seems to him that he is the only living person to escape a frenzied gathering of display-window dummies.

He leans out over the rail and lets the night wind cool his temples. The inconstant glow from a porthole projects weird streaks of light on the dark waves.

Veins of gold in granite.
El Dorado.

In the sound of the waves, the young doctor hears the distant song of the buccaneers, blowing in on the night wind from bygone ages.

He passes his days in his cabin, writing on the ship's immaculate stationery: prescriptions for American ladies suffering from seasickness and for elderly gentlemen with liver trouble.

At night, when the jazz band falls silent, when the sea wind can be heard again, and when only the hoarse shouts of a few drunken planters emerge from the smoking lounge, his heart comes alive with the madness of El Dorado.

In the night his good shirt, his tuxedo, his social position are all forgotten.

He feels a kinship with his ancestors, the savage raiders who hoarded gold in the holds of their ships, a kinship with the adventurers, the destroyers, the slave hunters.

Under the gray ashes of the daily grind, that same madness glows in the heart of every young white man: the feverish desire for El Dorado.

In 1499, Alonso de Ojeda and Juan de la Cosa reached the coast of the Guianas. Around the same time, Vicente Yáñez Pinzón discovered the mouth of the Amazon and the eastern Guianas. A rumor spread that far inland, a country had been discovered with immeasurable troves of gold and precious stones, and that the sandy shores of one infinitely large lake, named Parima, consisted entirely of gold dust.

Tempted by these rumors, Domingo de Vera undertook a voyage to the Guianas in 1593, claiming the territory for Spain with great ceremony on April 23, 1594. Commanders and soldiers knelt before a cross and offered up their thanks to heaven. "Then Domingo de Vera took a cup of water and drank from it; he took a second cup and poured it out, scattering the liquid as far as he could, drew his sword, and cut the grass around him, as well as a few branches from the trees, saying, 'In the name of God, I take possession of this country for His Majesty Don Philip, our lawful overlord!'"[6]

This is also the earliest example of the misuse of God's name in the colonial tragedy. It was often said later, in Christian books, that the Negro is not human, because humans are made in God's image and, after all, those Bible scholars added, God is not black ...

So let us, here, as Negroes, offer this assurance: we agree we were not created in the image of the God whose blessing was always invoked by those early white colonists, whenever they seized the land, bodies, and belongings of people of other colors.

The high expectations of the Spanish gold-seekers never became a reality. As no gold was found in the coastal areas, it was assumed that the natives were hiding it in the hinterlands. With their weapons in hand, they forced their way into the hinterland, and wherever opposition was found, the whites used bloodhounds, whose names have gone down in history.

Yet El Dorado was never found.

And the embittered adventurers vented their wrath on the natives, depriving them of their freedom, binding them in chains, forcing them to labor, flogging them, and abusing them.

And when that race proved too weak to bring forth the treasures that the whites, in their frenzy, had believed would be theirs for the taking – when, beaten and abused, they died by the thousands – the Spanish in Suriname recalled the advice of Las Casas to import a stronger race than the Indians from Africa.[7]

It was then that the slave trade began.

It was in those days that the first of our ancestors were brought to Suriname.

From that time onward, slavery in Suriname took shape. Each new ruler drove out the last, yet each one, after taking violent possession of the settlements of other Europeans, would begin by making the solemn declaration that under the new regime the right of property – which is to say, the right to use and abuse one's living chattels, to buy and sell our fathers and mothers – would still be held sacred and enforced.

The First Settlements

Despite the ceremonious occupation of Suriname by the Spaniards, their power was hardly in evidence. They were soon driven out of the Guianas by the constant attacks of wrathful Indians. By this time, the French, as well as the

Hollanders and Zeelanders, had begun to ply the coast of the Guianas more regularly. A Dutch General Charter of 1614 awarded anyone who discovered any new harbor, passage, or site the right to use it exclusively for four years. Yet still there were no long-term settlements. The Europeans first gained a foothold in the Guianas in the mid seventeenth century. Captain Maréchal, accompanied by sixty English settlers, established a colony along the river dubbed the "Suriname," but no other historical facts about this settlement have come to light. In 1643, a company was founded in Rouen for the colonization of Suriname. A man named Charles Poncet de Brétigny led a band of fortune-hunters that settled on the coast. But they treated the Indians so brutally that they were eventually chased out, and some were put to death. A few years later, a different French company made a new attempt at colonization, sending eight hundred French colonists, but this did not lead to a lasting presence either.

The French were followed by the British. In 1650, Baron Willoughby of Parham outfitted a ship for a voyage to Guyana at his own expense. The ship received a friendly welcome from the natives, because its crew pretended to be merchants who came in peace. It soon became clear, however, that these pacifists were in fact stern soldiers, who drove the Indians into the forest with their superior weapons. They hurried to build strong forts that could withstand the attacks of the cheated, vengeful natives. In 1652, Baron Willoughby came to Suriname in person to take up the leadership of the new colony. But he did not stay for long. Soon afterwards he was appointed governor of the West Indian islands and departed for Barbados, leaving a certain Ruff in charge in Suriname. Thus Europe had gained a foothold in Suriname and established its dominion; the situation had changed forever.

Furthermore, this situation was confirmed by law in 1662, by a letter from Charles II granting the coast and territory of Suriname to Lord Francis Willoughby, Baron of Parham, and to Lawrence Hyde, the son of the Earl of Clarendon, and to their progeny and lawful heirs.

Under the English regime, the number of whites in Suriname swiftly increased, mainly because of the many Jews from Cayenne who settled in Suriname in 1664 under the leadership of David Nassy. Willoughby granted them equal rights and liberties to the English. In short order, under the iron rule of the English, more than sixty sugar and tobacco plantations were established by the red and black slaves. This hard labor in the tropical heat was tiring beyond words and cost many slaves their lives. The others, in their misery, consoled themselves with firewater, which was imported by the whites for the first time in those days. The indigenous Surinamers soon decreased in number and retreated into the forest, from where they made occasional doomed attempts to drive out the foreigners. The black slaves, too, were stricken with disease or died of exhaustion. No matter. The slave traders provided a regular supply; the trade in human beings flourished!

The Dutch Regime

The Spaniards had made the first voyages of discovery, the French the first attempt at colonization. The British had conquered the country, built forts, and established plantations, and their relatively liberal policies (toward other whites) enabled them to attract competent Jewish settlers to their colony. The Dutch did not appear on the scene until a comfortable bed had been prepared for them. Did they bring a new level of civilization to the colony?

Since 1661, the Republic of the United Netherlands had been at war with England. In order to do the greatest possible damage to the enemy in all places, the States of Zeeland outfitted three warships manned by three hundred soldiers and commanded by Abraham Crijnssen, Philip Julius Lichtenberg, and Maurits de Rama. On February 26, 1667, this squadron sailed up the Suriname River under the English flag. Yes, it was under the *English* flag that the Dutch made their first approach to their future possession. Although this ruse was unsuccessful because they were unfamiliar with the English signals, the fort was so poorly prepared for an attack that after only a brief skirmish it fell to the Dutch. Most of the colonists were granted a continuation of the privileges awarded them by the English. Yet to the winner go the spoils: Governor William Byam's goods were confiscated, and the colonists were forced to pay a levy of hundreds of thousands of pounds of sugar.[8] The total revenue for the Zeelanders from these confiscations was more than four hundred thousand guilders, proof that Suriname was already a prospering colony by then.

The fort was reinforced with new defensive works and a garrison of 120 men was left there under the command of Maurits de Rama and furnished with fifteen artillery pieces, food, and other military supplies. In 1667, the Peace of Breda traded the Dutch colony of New Netherland to England in return for Suriname, the very same way a wagonload of billy goats is swapped for a wagonload of sheep.

But peace treaties and all such solemn promises must be enjoyed with a grain of salt. The Peace of Breda was signed on July 31, 1667, but as soon as October 18 of that year, the English admiral John Harman arrived at Fort Zeelandia with seven warships. Mere months after the Dutch reinforcements, the fort fell back into British hands. The Dutch Republic protested against the attack to the English government, which gave orders to evacuate the colony. What followed was no less than an exodus. More than 1,200 of the English left the colony, taking with them large quantities of slaves, cattle, and goods, and settled in Jamaica.

In 1674, the Peace of Westminster made a definitive transfer of sovereignty over Suriname to the Republic of the United Netherlands.

This business had an aftermath, however. Under English rule, a number of agreements had been concluded with the indigenous people, but it never occurred to the Dutch to uphold those agreements. On the contrary, they drove the inhabitants ever further from their land, which they acquired through so-called sales contracts in exchange for assorted rubbish such as blades, mirrors, and fishing tackle. This explains why the Indians revolted again, in the hope of freeing themselves from the foreign yoke. Although they did not wage a regular war with a large military force, they did attack plantations in small bands, killing many white people. The colonists were virtually defenseless against these courageous Surinamese people, whose familiarity with the terrain gave them a huge advantage over the whites. Even a force of one hundred and fifty troops, Zeelanders armed to the teeth, led against them in the field under Governor Heinsius (1680), returned home unsuccessful. We, the Surinamese of today, remember and honor these forefathers.

The history of the arrival of the Dutch in our country would not be complete without mention of the sordid quarrel between Zeeland and the States General, which wrangled over the possession of Suriname like dogs over a bone.[9] Since Crijnssen, who held Fort Zeelandia, was a Zeelander, his heroic courage gave the States of Zeeland a claim to sovereign authority. But the States General had a more compelling case; they had paid for the expedition.

This dispute went unsettled. Zeeland remained in provisional possession of Suriname, while the States General were acknowledged as holding a kind of supreme authority. But, when the uprisings by the indigenous people took ever more extreme forms under Heinsius, both the States of Zeeland and the States General were content to transfer this dangerous expense item to the honorable West India Company (West-Indische Compagnie; WIC). The States of Zeeland received 260,000 guilders in return, and the States General granted the new owners a ten-year charter.

In this thirty-two-article charter (a sort of Constitution for Suriname), the civilizing mission of the Dutch as the colonial power in Suriname was given the form of a monopolistic commercial business.

Since the colonists had no intention of giving up their beloved fatherland forever to earn their bread by the sweat of their brow in the tropical sun, their prosperity depended on a swift and ready influx of usable slaves. The monopoly on supplying these beasts of burden was obtained by the West India Company. In the exact words of Article VI of the charter, "That since the aforementioned Colony cannot adequately be sustained other than by Black Slaves, or Negroes, and since no one other than the said Company has the competence in these Territories to import slaves from the coast of Africa, the sole place of the trade in them, the said Company shall be obligated to deliver annually such numbers of slaves to the aforementioned Colony as shall be required there."[10]

To put the business in a slightly better light, the West India Company also assumed the obligation to ensure "that the Colonists shall at all times be furnished with one or more Ministers of the Holy Word, for the purpose of instructing the Colonists and the other inhabitants in the fear of the Lord and the Doctrine of Salvation."[11]

But the colony had fallen into decline because of the English exodus and the Indian attacks, and the West India Company, which already had its best days behind it, could not afford the investments needed to make it profitable again. So, in 1683, it sold one-third of its rights to the city of Amsterdam and one-third to Cornelis van Aerssen van Sommelsdijck, who was appointed governor by the deed of transfer. The new owners took the name of the Chartered Society of Suriname. But supreme sovereignty and responsibility for defense remained with the States General.

Essentially, this transfer changed nothing. The West India Company kept its monopoly on the slave trade, except that the Chartered Society obtained the right to import slaves as well if necessary, on condition that it paid fifteen guilders (in import duties, as we would call them) to the West India Company.

The Slave Trade

On the boundless deep blue of the ocean sails a frigate, sublime in the taut pomp of its stays and shrouds, in the vaulting white of its wind-swollen sails. No pounding machines propel it, no clouds of black smoke besmirch the blue dome of the heavens. Seen from the crow's nest, the ship below us resembles a white fish; sea-froth splashes the bowsprit; two sailors at the helm sing an old, old sea shanty.

No spectacle matches that of a square-rigged three-master in full sail; it is finer than Hauser's "last sailing ship," finer than the frigate *Johanna Maria*, it is the dream of those who, amid the noise of the big city, amid typewriters and calculating machines, dream of the golden plenitude of bygone ages.[12]

We do not begrudge you your imagined seat in the crow's nest of that old ship. We do not begrudge you the sea wind through your hair and the song of the sailors below you, who belt out a tune from the yards as they lower the topgallant sails.

But we do wish to warn you. From your lofty seat, do not venture down the futtock shroud, or even take the less dangerous route through the lubber's hole. Do not set foot on the rope ladders that lead to the poop deck, however white and freshly scrubbed they may appear from here on high.

Up here you can smell the invigorating odor of tar and the salt sea wind.

Down there it already reeks a mile leeward of the sweat and excrement of a thousand slaves packed into the hold.

Up here you hear the cry of the albatross, the song of the sailors, and the crash of the waves.

Down there you hear the cries of the slaves, the wails of a woman in labor, and the crack of the whip coming down on the backs of the blacks.

You will not take any pleasure in what lies below decks, the squalid breeding grounds of filth and vermin where the men and women – separated, all chained up, then packed together to save space – cry out their despair. You too must sense some part of the despair and sorrow of the blacks, dragged out of their homes, far from their families, seasick and malnourished, full of dread at their unknown destination.

In any case, a trip below deck is not entirely free of danger. Sometimes a slave goes into a frenzy, attacking his guards, in the hope of being struck dead. It has even happened that all the slaves on a ship rose up in revolt. We know this took place on a slave ship from Zeeland, the *Middelburgs Welvaren*, in 1751.

Two or three days after the ship left the African coast for Guyana, the slaves rose up against their bestial treatment by the whites. Without weapons, they tried to oppose the heavily armed crew. We are told that out of two hundred and sixty slaves only thirty survived, while the white crew "were fortunate enough not to lose a single man."[13]

The Market

A good salesman always sees to it that his wares look their best before putting them on the market! And whatever the Dutchmen lacked in humanity, they were always good salesmen; we must grant them that.

Before the abducted Negroes were embarked in Africa, these slaves, our fathers, were placed in a warehouse inside the fortress built to protect this abominable trade. There they were allowed to spend all day outdoors, in a little yard in the open air, and they were rubbed with oil so that their bodies would glisten and excite interest in the marketplace. During this interlude, they were also given plenty of food, so that their famished appearance would not scare off the buyers. Every evening after sundown, they were lined up and driven into the warehouses, where they remained until the next morning. Finally, they were brought before the director-general, one by one, where they were carefully examined by European surgeons. The results of this examination separated the "deliverables" from the "undeliverables," a group that included slaves who looked older than thirty-five, as well as those who were maimed or proved to be ill. If they were missing teeth or had gray hair, they were classified among the cheaper varieties.

Next, the deliverables were lined up and registered and then, just like livestock, branded on their chests with a hot iron that seared the company name or coat of arms into their skin.[14]

When the slave ship had reached Suriname and the wares were looking reasonable again after a few days of relatively good food, the poor Negro slaves were washed and then rubbed with oil and grease, and all sorts of figures, such as stars, half-moons, and others, were shaved into their head so that they would be exposed to the mockery and derision of the then so highly civilized white race.

After that the auction could begin.

There is no denying it: the Dutch are good merchants. And why wouldn't they increase their profits by exploiting the natural properties with which God happened to endow human beings, even those in black skins?

Even a black man has a certain attachment to his wife and family. If the black man is sold without his family, the buyer runs a serious risk of loss, because the "damned nigger" may be quick to flee in the hope of finding his family. The gentlemen of the Company know this, so they are careful to auction off a man and his family in separate lots, to motivate the buyer of the man to pay for the second lot with his wife and children as well.

The Company merchant surveys his wares with satisfaction. To be sure, prices may rise and fall a little as they do in any trade, depending on the number of slaves imported, but a strong, healthy Negro always fetches a decent price. And they were healthy and strong, our fathers, before the poisonous firewater destroyed their constitutions, before the germs of malaria took root in their undernourished bodies. Healthy and strong and beautiful they were, those children of nature, among whom physical defects were a rare exception.

Now, as the sale is about to begin, the interested parties are invited in. The slaves, our fathers, are forced to jump, run, and smile on command. They were advised beforehand to be friendly so that they will find good masters.

A white fellow subjects a pretty ten-year-old girl to a shameless examination. Yesterday her mother was sold privately by the dealer.

A cruel-looking European grabs a Negro by the chin and pulls open his mouth to check the condition of the teeth. The slave is made to show off his arm muscles and to hop, step, and jump as proof that there is nothing wrong with his legs. And all around the wares on display, the spectators gather, poking at the bodies and discussing the quality of the goods, as uninhibited as buyers at a cattle market.

Then the official auction begins.

One by one or in lots, the slaves are brought to the block, where the auctioneer shouts out their good qualities, often in the form of a crude, offensive joke.

A quick skirmish begins between the bidders.

"Mine."

And the slave is handed over to his new owner, who takes him to the brander to have the first letters of his name burned into his new slave's skin.

The second brand.

This is how the slave begins his life in Sranan.

Enslaved

I [Pinson Bonham] have spent 21 years in the West Indies, and in every colony I have always heard that it was a very severe punishment for a Negro to sell him to a planter in Suriname, and I now discover this to be true.[15]

I have never yet been in a colony where the slaves were so ill-treated, so ill-fed and ill-clothed, yet where they were forced to do such heavy labor, far exceeding their powers.[16]

Letters from Bonham to Earl Bathurst

For centuries, the white experts in matters of religion went to great lengths to prove that slavery was an institution ordained by God – "that there can be no doubt it was the will of Providence for the African people to be servants and be kept in a state of subjection." After all, in the words of Scripture, "Cursed be Canaan, a servant of servants shall he be unto his brethren."[17]

And the Reverend Johan Picardt, a late minister in Coevoerden, wrote, "These people [the Africans, whom he regarded as descendants of Ham, destined for slavery] are so constituted by nature that if set at liberty or treated with affection they will not behave themselves and cannot even keep themselves under control, but all those who are persistently caned in the limbs and bastinadoed without mercy can be expected to render good service; therefore their welfare derives from slavery."[18]

Sure enough, the practice of "bastinado" soon bore fruit: namely, the rich profits that Suriname yielded for the whites in those days.

In 1730 the number of plantations was around 400. Their crops included sugar, coffee, cocoa, and tobacco. In 1749 more than 30,000 pounds of tobacco was sent to Holland, and in only one year a single plantation could export 20,000 pounds of cotton and 50,000 pounds of coffee.

These figures speak for themselves.

And yet, even if devout ministers wrote that "Providence saw fit, did it not, to condemn the race of Negroes to slavery centuries ago," one still might ask whether Providence really intended for slavery in Suriname to show such marks of barbaric cruelty.

All labor in Suriname was performed by slaves driven to it by beating. What other incitement could have led them to do their work properly? Wages were unheard of throughout Suriname, unless you care to use that term for their vermin-infested hovels, their meager diet. Nor did slaves enjoy the satisfaction of working to provide for their families. Instead, they knew all their toil could not prevent their families from being torn apart at their master's whim the very next day, or whenever he chose to sell them or their wives or children to another planter, or to gamble them away at dice, as many planters did.

Those slaves, our fathers, toiled in the fields to increase the wealth of the whites. On the sugar plantations, where the slaves in the fields were worked to exhaustion and death, the Europeans stood behind them with whips, ready to lash their naked bodies at the slightest hint that they were slowing down. At harvest time, they were often not even permitted to sleep at night.

On the timber estates, the men and women toiled together, felling the trees and sawing them into boards. As a rule, the unfortunate women were responsible for transporting the boards and lumber on their heads from the forest to the landing.

Maybe you, white reader, learned at school that the Mauritshuis in The Hague was made of the most precious varieties of Brazilian wood. As you pause to marvel at this building, we ask that you think of how it was for our mothers, who bore those heavy burdens on their heads day in and day out (because Sunday was one institution that the Christian civilizers neglected to introduce in Suriname), lugging them across hilly terrain, through pools and swamps, always under the threat of the whips wielded by your ancestors.

So, I hardly need add that disease and coughing up blood were everyday events. The enslaved men and women on these timber estates did not remain usable for long, and the business manager knew they would wear out fast. This creaky clockwork was lubricated with the rotgut spirits supplied now and then by the master so that his slaves, for the span of their brief intoxication, would forget their misery.

We wish to support these claims with a few facts, just a page or two from the black book of Surinamese cruelty.

We are told that under the regime of Governor Mauricius, the public prosecutor brought charges against one Miss Pieterson, who had a reputation for inhuman cruelty. When her house was searched, it came to light that she had *"taken the lives* of a multitude of her slaves *in tyrannical and barbaric ways."* She did not dream of denying these acts, but told the investigating committee with pride "that she had the right to destroy her own goods, purchased with her own money."[19]

But the colonial justice system did not punish her; she found time to flee first.

The Widow Mauricius, a member of Suriname's upper crust, had an old slave woman tied to a tree and beaten to death. By her own declaration, she did so on a whim, because she wanted to see her former nursemaid suffer. Various other slaves of hers had suffered the same fate; yes, even the little children on her plantation often received the punishment known as the "Spanish billy goat" (a highly refined form of torture, discussed below).

The widow's slaves then informed the Colonial Court that they would desert the plantation if the governor's widow was not removed as its manager.

The Court did try to persuade her to relinquish control of the plantation to an administrator, "because it was feared that she might otherwise bring utter ruin to the belongings of her wards." But Mrs. Mauricius made it known that no one else could better manage her *property* than she herself.

On another occasion, she declared, "I don't want any Negro of mine going about my plantation with such a smooth hide." In fact, she had devised an efficient method of weight loss, which almost always worked: she sometimes had all her slaves tortured and "half skinned or flayed" for twenty-four hours without interruption. One Negro man and two Negro women died as a result of this treatment. The committee later dispatched to her plantation reported that "the slaves looked very bad and abused."[20]

No wonder a number of the widow's slaves fled and sought refuge with the rebellious maroons in the forest. The same thing was attempted by a few of the slaves of Mrs. La Parra, a mistress who outdid the Widow Mauricius in cruelty.

But, while fleeing into the forest, these slaves fell into the hands of the colonial justice system. Three of them, two men and one woman, were hanged, while three of the men and four of the women were subjected to the "Spanish billy goat" on the scaffold for fleeing unlawfully. As for Mrs. La Parra, she received a reprimand from the colonial justice authorities, who admonished her "to treat her slaves in a more moderate and orderly manner" from then on.[21]

But reprimands of that kind were rare – and in truth, it was rarer still that such an attack led to an investigation and a written record of the facts. Cruelty toward slaves was then so customary that it had to take very exceptional forms to be recorded in the colonial chronicles.[22] More than in the history books of the whites, the abuse of our fathers is recorded in our own hearts. Never have the sufferings of slavery spoken to me so clearly as through the eyes of my grandmother when, in front of the hut in Paramaribo, she told us children her tales of the old days.

Even after slavery had been abolished in French Guiana, many Dutch colonists went on committing the most scandalous cruelties. The director C. Varenhorst worked his slaves half to death and deprived them of even a bare minimum of food. On a mere suspicion, he had a slave severely beaten, put him in fetters, and chained him to a pole by the neck. Varenhorst then forbade all his other slaves to come to the assistance of their shackled friend, on pain of punishment. The slave soon died for lack of food and water and because of his terrible pain, "in stench and decay." This case was taken to the Colonial Court of Holland. But that institution, whose task was surely to administer justice in accordance with law and equity, decided in Varenhorst's favor, and the plaintiffs received the "Spanish billy goat."[23]

Even as late as 1801, slaves were hanged or broken on the wheel by judicial sentence almost every month, and the "Spanish billy goat" was carried out almost every day, either on the scaffold or in Fort Zeelandia. The situation was so intolerable that the soldiers complained, saying this "almost daily spectacle" was "disagreeable and repugnant."[24]

The Slave Woman

Mother dear, far away from this cold country where I am writing, Mother dear in Suriname, with your gray hair, with your frame bowed before its time, to you who toiled and labored from morning to night so that I could have an education, to you I dedicate this darkest chapter in our history.

When the male slaves, our fathers, returned from the fields at sunset after finishing work for the day, they had until early morning to recover from their fatigue, they had their wretched huts in which to stretch their aching limbs on their beds of rags and rest until the overseer called them back to work.

But when the last line of women returned home through the fields carrying heavy baskets of cotton on their heads, it often happened that the eye of the master (or in later times the administrator) would fall upon one of the young Negro women, and he would beckon her to put down her basket. That night, she would have a second job: satisfying her master's lascivious lusts. There was no form of exemption from this duty. Since Negro slaves were not, after all, human, neither the sacraments of the Church nor the laws of the citizenry applied to them. A patata (white) simply could not believe that there could be anything like a marriage bond between two blacks, and even married slave women had to go repeatedly from their marital beds to their master's house.

We must admit that a white master sometimes showered his black favorite with all sorts of special favors, as well as silk clothes and even jewels, whether on a whim or to make his acquaintances on other plantations jealous of her beauty. This made it all the more regrettable what became of those mistresses when, after a short while, they no longer charmed their master. Then they returned to their hovels in the slave quarter, showered no longer with love but with hatred, no longer with favors but with abuse. The master's betrayed white spouse often seized the opportunity to vent her rage on the now defenseless victim.

As for the children of such liaisons, they were regarded simply as an addition to the human herd, and the lashes of their father's whip, or perhaps their white half-brother's, were meted out with complete impartiality, leaving scars just as deep on their backs as on those of their full-blooded kin. Simply note the number of mulattoes in Suriname and you will realize that the pretended aversion of the white race to the blacks has never formed an obstacle to sexual intercourse with our women!

Once again, we would like to start by presenting a few facts by way of example:

Mr. Pichot, a nephew of the public prosecutor of the same name and the director of Vlucht en Trouw Plantation, alarmed the entire white population in his vicinity on September 6, 1750, by announcing that his Negroes had risen up against him. It transpired that Mr. Pichot had wanted to lie with a certain slave woman, but she had staunchly refused to give in to her master's base passions. The poor slave woman was flogged to death by Pichot for her chastity, and when one old slave protested, Pichot "shot him full in the stomach with lead buckshot."[25]

There is also the case of the wealthy planter on Arendsrust Plantation. When he heard that one of his slaves was in love with his slave woman Betje, his own mistress, he had the slave flogged and burned all over his body and then nailed him into wooden shackles. After the poor persecuted man died of his injuries, he was tossed into a pit of quicklime. Betje, who had returned the slave's affections, was also tied up, flogged until she bled, and burned in a shameful and horrific manner.[26]

Under these circumstances, slaves could never know domestic happiness, since the white master always cast a menacing shadow between the two spouses.

European women sought to compensate for their white husbands' neglect by taking out their hatred on the beautiful Negro women who were their rivals, often with inhuman cruelty. Or such a woman might try to punish her white husband by having an affair with a white man who had recently arrived from Europe. Another despicable custom was to "charge beautiful slave women a weekly tax payable to their master or his wife, without knowing or seeking to learn how this money was earned or obtained."[27]

The targets of this forced prostitution were generally attractive Negro, mulatto, mestizo, quadroon, and kabugru women. If these women came down with the venereal disease imported from Europe, they were covered with red paint and paraded through the streets of the capital. Then they were left to their fate, to waste away in misery.

The Masters

... that there must be a slave class, bound to the heaviest, crushing labor and possessed of no more than an animal nature, and alongside it a higher, civilized class, which thereby has the means and the time to cultivate its intellect and perfect its powers, thus gaining command over the slaves.[28]

This was the theory, at any rate, that a leading public prosecutor shared with his family in Holland, and what better judge than an official of the colonial justice system! So let us once again underpin theory with fact, beginning with a sketch of the life of a white master on his plantation.

The master rose early in the morning, went to the yard in front of the house or the pleasure ground, lit a real Dutch pipe of fragrant Barinas tobacco, and then had one of his slave women devotedly serve him a cup of coffee.

While this white gentleman, respectable to the core, took the cool, refreshing morning air at his leisure, the white foreman arrived and, after the usual bows and ceremonies (an important part of his duties), he reported on the day before and received his orders for the working day ahead. He described at length what work had been performed by the slave men and women, whether any Negroes had left the plantation, which ones were ill or had died, and whether any births had taken place among them (a welcome expansion of the herd).

After this, the morning took on a grimmer tone, with a list of the slave men and women who, as the foreman saw it, had not performed their duties adequately the day before, who had stopped for a little rest or committed some other transgression.

The foreman acted as the prosecutor, the master as the judge, and a specially trained slave carried out the sentence without delay.[29] If the blows happened to land a little too forcefully, endangering the slave's value as a worker for the day, then, fortunately, the dresiman was also present: another slave who – with no training whatsoever, of course – had been made responsible for the health of the slaves.

The dresiman, too, made his report, and it was always good news for him when the situation was only mildly disappointing and he came away with no worse than a hearty Dutch curse. But he was often flogged along with the culprits when, in the master's opinion, too many slaves were malingering. The dresiman was appointed not to treat the ill, but to decide which ones could be chased out of their sick beds to work without danger to their lives (because that would mean loss of property).

The next to report for duty was "the mama," an old slave woman responsible for supervising the plantation's Negro children, because the Dutch were extremely modern back then and had a day-care system, so that mothers could go off to work without a second thought. From this perspective, one might even see slavery as laying the groundwork for the emancipation of Negro women!

Yet enough bitter irony. The mama reported for duty, bringing along the whole stock of Negro children (for in the eyes of the master they were nothing but livestock to be yoked to his plows in due course). All the children had been bathed beforehand and had the privilege of being fed a little rice and plantain in the presence of their august protector. Then, with an obligatory grimace of gratitude, they were permitted to leave. Only the mama remained. And woe to her if she had the death of a slave child to report. In most cases, she then had to say farewell to this world, for terrible is the master's wrath when the death of a young slave deprives him of his property.

When these tiring tasks have been completed, the master decides to take his morning walk – or rather, since the tropical sun is already scorching, to mount his horse and go out riding.

He is dressed in fine linen trousers, silk stockings, red or yellow shoes, a silk shirt, and a wide beaver hat. A slave accompanies him with a large parasol to protect him from the burning sun.

At a leisurely gait, he crosses the lush fields, where the plants seem to grow all the better the more they are fertilized with Negro blood. In the meantime, his eyes dart about in search of careless slaves who have laid down their work for a moment or dared to lift their eyes from the ground.

After returning from this morning exercise, the gentleman takes his breakfast and dresses a second time, as was the custom in those days, this time as a fop or dandy.

If the planter was of a mind to visit friends or neighbors, he wended his way to his gilded rowboat, which was loaded down with fruit, wine, gin, and tobacco. While he sat back and relaxed, eight sturdy slaves rowed him to his destination. If the master had no wish to go out, then he would have breakfast somewhat later and take more time to linger over it. He did not breakfast on rice and plantain as the Negro children did; instead, his table was laden with fine ham, salted meat, roast chicken or pigeon, plantain, casaba, bread, cream, butter, and cheese, and he drank strong beer or French wine.

Then the planter took his afternoon nap and, afterwards, returned to the table for the finest dishes available in those days.

In the evening, rum and punch were drunk, Barinas tobacco was smoked, and the dice game hazard was played. This wearying intellectual work usually went on until deep in the night.

Europe's institutions of higher learning teach that the Greek temples were built by slaves, that that whole astonishing culture with all its sublime philosophical and poetic creations, its marvelous paintings and sculptures, its plays, music, and dance, could exist only because an army of slaves gave its rulers the opportunity to be civilized and free.

We leave to professional scholars the question of whether this thesis is correct, or whether, when the Greeks began importing slaves (which required a certain prior level of power and wealth), it marked the beginning of the decline of a culture whose exalted principles were irreconcilable with the unjust practice of slavery.

Nor do we intend to ask whether the nature of this ancient household slavery – as different from the Surinamese variety as the treatment of a beloved steed by its master is different from the treatment of an old nag by a hackney coach company – may have been more compatible with the basic principles of human decency.

Yet we *are* entitled to ask this question of you, people of the Netherlands: If slavery is the foundation of culture, what temples have you built in Suriname? What poems have you written? What lofty ideas have you handed down to posterity? Wouldn't you be at a loss if you had to erect even one single statue in Suriname for Dutch colonists famed for their intellectual achievements?

At best, you could cast the likenesses in bronze of a few military men who captured the villages of maroon rebels with their modern weaponry – a Vaillant, a Mayland, Creutz, and Nepveu. But even then you would have to acknowledge that your most capable governors and the warriors who defended you always had to be imported from Europe, because the class of Surinamese property owners degenerated too rapidly, through luxury and extravagance, to bring forth competent individuals themselves. No, if you wish to erect a statue, dedicate it to the chefs who cooked such magnificent meals under Governor Spörcke or Crommelin and to whom that era owes its fame, or to the coach builders who made magnificent carriages so that European ladies could ride through the streets of Paramaribo.

And yet Suriname did possess, if any place did, the economic basis for building a culture.

It was no rarity for thirty to fifty slaves to be present in the master's mansion, for his personal service alone.

In the late eighteenth century, a new system was widely adopted: plantation owners entrusted the management of their plantations, which they called their "securities," to white administrators, who received an annual income of seventy to eighty thousand guilders for their work and an additional forty to fifty thousand for taking over duties in the colonial administration.

In those days, Suriname made three hundred million guilders in annual revenue from sugar, coffee, and cotton alone. The freight paid to Dutch ships, which always took on impressive loads in Suriname, was approximately one million. In 1787 alone, Suriname produced twenty-five thousand barrels of sugar, fifteen million pounds of coffee, three million pounds of cotton, one million pounds of cocoa, 250,000 kilograms of tobacco, and so forth.[30]

In those days slaves were sold privately and used up completely. But it was a rarity to see a book in the hands of a white person. The establishment of a theater in 1775 (which did not remain open long) was regarded as a great cultural milestone. And one Dutch writer, no less than Governor Mauricius, offered the flattering testimony to his compatriots that "there is no denying the crude and obscene ways of life among the Europeans in Suriname" and that many white colonists "have no occupation but sleeping, boozing, gambling, and doing evil."[31]

And the English author J.G. Stedman, who spent a few years in Suriname, wrote, "Luxury and dissipation in this Country are carried to the extreme and in my opinion must send Thousands to the Grave, the Men are generally a set of poor wither'd mortals – as dry and sapless as a squeesed lemon – owing to their intemperate way of living ..."[32]

Wolbers makes a telling remark in his history of Suriname: "Forgive us, dear reader, for reporting specifics from what Mauricius rightly called an 'abyss of obscenities'. It is a sad thing for a writer to have to keep recounting the sins and flaws of the people whose history he ventures to sketch, yet he must not let this stand in the way of truthfulness, however dearly he may wish he could tell of greater and nobler deeds."[33]

The white population reached the pinnacle of their civilization in their festivities.

Frans Hals's militia pieces still display the wild extravagance of these revelries, which were elevated almost to an art form.

The feasts held in the palatial headquarters of the colonial administration in Paramaribo fell short of their Dutch models only in one way: the contented flush of the Dutch regents was absent from the sallow white faces of the Surinamese slaveholders.

In every other respect, the extravagance and luxury were as much larger in scale and more provocative as Suriname is larger than Holland.

Rows of slaves as servants,
golden plates and cutlery,
the glitter of jewelry,
silk garments.

It was as if the revelers were trying to forget, in a frenzy of sensual pleasure, the fear of the downtrodden in every heart, as if they hoped this spectacle of carefree dissipation would impress the slaves in the dining hall and the silent black masses.

And late in the tropical night, they set off screeching fireworks, as if shooing up to the stars the surplus of luxury that could not be squandered fast enough down below.

The Punishments

"Hunger is a sharp sword," a Dutch proverb tells us, but fear has always been a sharper sword than hunger.

The Surinamese propertied class may dance in the colonial headquarters until they drop; they know they are dancing on the rim of a volcano.

They know the bitter resentment of that black multitude outside the windows, even if they do not understand the language spoken in the huts of the slaves.

They know that the camel's back, heaped with straw upon straw, sometimes unexpectedly breaks, that slaves sometimes suddenly revolt against their white masters.

They know that in the forest there dwells an implacable army of maroons, whom no promise can purchase, no force oppress.

The fear of a general slave revolt – as well as the fear of their own conscience, of acknowledging the undeniable fact that a person oppressed remains a human being – occupies the hearts of the oppressors, poisoning their quiet moments, making them reach for the mug and the game board, permeating their minds and turning their thoughts to ever harsher, ever crueler punishments.

Among the punishments that were the customary preroga-
tives of the master, one of the foremost was the so-called
"Spanish billy goat." This punishment involved tying the
slave's two hands together, pulling the knees up through
the arms, and then inserting a stick between the tied hands
and the raised knees. This stick was planted firmly in the
ground, and then came the flogging with a bundle of rods
(made of tamarind, a very hard and knotty wood). Once
the slave had been beaten through and through on the
exposed upper side, until his flesh was completely raw, he
was turned over so that the other side could receive the
same treatment. Sometimes these floggings were instead
administered with iron staves, but since that form of
punishment generally resulted in death, and therefore the
loss of the slaveholders' property, they did not make a
habit of it.

The whites in Paramaribo were spared the unpleasant
task of administering this variety of discipline; they could
leave their slaves with the jailer of Fort Zeelandia. He and
his assistants were specially trained in this craft, and in
exchange for a substantial tip they were happy to put in
some extra effort.

At the master's request, this "Spanish billy goat"
punishment was inflicted in public at whatever series of
intersections he chose. This gave rise to expressions such
as the "four-corner" or "seven-corner Spanish billy goat."

Plantation owners further from the capital, unlike their
more fortunate compatriots in the city, could not make
use of the jailer's services, but this did not prevent them
from applying the convenient punishment known as
bastinado. They were empowered by law to administer
"eighty lashes of the whip," which were among the
so-called "ordinary plantation punishments." But – in
the words of Governor Crommelin – "it was not specified
whether the slave was to receive the lashes in an unbound

or a suspended state,[34] *and it is in any case well known that slaves, when tied up and stretched out, die after many fewer lashes*; and that meanwhile such evil incidents are increasing in number by the day, and always under the pretext (should they ever come to light) that the death was not caused by the lashes and beatings but followed them by chance."[35]

The Governing Council[36]

The legal system likewise meted out the cruelest of punishments in those days. Heavy flogging, the "seven-way Spanish billy goat," and branding on both shoulders were classified "as not being severe punishments" (from a judgment of February 25, 1740).

The Governing Council sentenced a slave named Kwaku, who had resisted a white officer, to be bound to a pole, flogged severely, and branded, after which his foot was to be chopped off.[37]

The slave Pedro, who had fled his master, was taken captive and sentenced to have one leg chopped off, and to a lifetime of hard labor on the fortifications.[38]

A few slaves who had been accused of theft received the "seven-way Spanish billy goat" and were also branded on both cheeks. Then pieces were cut off their ears.[39]

The death penalty took the form of hanging or breaking at the wheel. A third frequent form of this penalty was hanging the slave on a hook. The hook was stabbed through the skin or under the ribs, and as if even that excruciating pain were not enough, the punishment was made still worse by applying red-hot tongs to the fleshy parts. Nor was it exceptional in those days to burn slaves alive.

When maroons were put on trial, such cruelty was boundless. One example from among the many monstrous sentences in the historical record: in 1730, after Captain Swallenberg, having captured several maroon villages, brought back eleven prisoners of war as spoils, the Governing Council imposed the following punishments:

A Negro named Joosje was pierced through the ribs with an iron hook, by which he was suspended from the gallows with his head and feet dangling. He must have been in unbearable pain, but he showed no sign of it. After he died, his head was chopped off and displayed on an iron pike; the rest of his body was left for birds to prey on.

The Negroes Wirai and Manbote were bound to poles and burned alive over a small pyre; all the while, their flesh was pinched at intervals with red-hot tongs. Only ashes remained.

The negresses Lucretia, Ambia, Agia, Gomba, Maria, and Victoria were bound to crosses and then broken alive on the wheel, and after they were executed, their heads were chopped off and also mounted on pikes by the waterside. The negresses Diana and Christina simply had their heads chopped off with an axe and also exhibited there.[40]

We wish to supply a few more examples of how justice was administered, which shed a damning light on the rightfulness of colonial justice in those days.

One slave, who was called Darius, submitted complaints to the Council regarding the monstrous treatment of the slaves by Director Bongaard of Sinabo Plantation. An investigation was conducted and, according to the final report, the planter had ordered that a slave suspected of "handling poison" be flogged while suspended, then subjected to the "Spanish billy goat," and finally kept tied up in a carpentry shed. Bongaard forbade everyone to tend to the poor slave or give him food or drink. The slave died in intense pain; his body was tossed into the nearby creek.

Another slave was tortured in the same way but survived, upon which the planter had him strangled.

After the colonial justice authorities had heard the Darius case, they issued an urgent warning to all slaves on Sinabo Plantation to, before all else, obey their master in all things. Then they ordered that the complainant Darius, at his master's request, be subjected to the "Spanish billy goat." In the interest of justice, however, the Council also reprimanded Director Bongaard, telling him that "if his slaves ever committed such serious crimes again in the future, he should surrender them to the justice system instead of punishing them on his own authority."[41]

Claas Badouw, the director of La Rencontre Plantation, falsely accused his slave Pierro of attempting to poison him. Pierro was brought to the cookhouse, where his ten fingers and ten toes were chopped off with a sharp chisel. He was then forced to eat them. After that, Badouw himself took a knife and cut off one of the slave's ears, again making him eat it. Then the white gentleman cut off Pierro's tongue with a razor blade and ordered him to swallow it. Pierro, dying of agony, stammered a few sounds with the stump of his tongue. This sent Badouw into such a rage that he used a pair of tongs to tear out what remained of the tongue. Pierro was then taken to the riverside and tied to an old covered rowboat, and his tormentors tried to burn him alive by setting dry kantras alight. When the kantras would not catch fire, Badouw ordered that the poor slave be released, thoroughly flogged, and buried alive in a pit. And just as that beacon of civilization had ordered, so it came to pass.

Badouw's sole punishment was to be dismissed as director and banished from the country.[42]

On a few rare occasions, even the Dutch justice system appears to have decided that things had gone too far. In the trial of Cornelia Mulder, the wife of W. Celis, the public prosecutor remarked to the court that "a few of the inhabitants here treat their slaves in very evil and monstrous ways, castigating and punishing them for petty mistakes and offenses so harshly that they die soon afterwards, if not immediately, of the excessive beating."[43]

The death sentence was the only thing to which the Dutch gradually began to see objections. At any rate, the colonial government began buying up slaves from masters who had sentenced them to death. The death sentence was then commuted to forced labor for life on public works. In the spirit of the proverb, "Harsh is my hand, but gentle my intent,"[44] these convicts first had their tongues cut off and were then castrated and had the coat of arms of Holland branded into their cheeks. In this condition, they had to work in chains for the rest of their days.[45]

But if there is an apex of Dutch justice, we would award that distinction to the decision on the claim made by a gentleman named Godefroy, who had the audacity to demand compensation from the colonial administration for twenty-eight slaves he had executed himself. The Council found for the claimant, and he received a grand total of 5,600 guilders![46]

In general, the white masters did not seem to see anything. They did not see the oppressed colored people when they began their toil each day in dawn's gray twilight. They saw nothing in those slaves but wretched, raggedy, accursed Negroes. They saw and heard neither the pain in their bodies nor the suffering in their hearts; they devoted no attention to hardship or abuse or the wailing of the victims. They gave all the more thought to the profits that the Company had to make.

The History of Our Nation

When we small Negro boys, the children or grandchildren of slaves, were taught "the History of our Nation" in school, it goes without saying that what we learned was the history of the white military men. The class was taught by the Brothers of Tilburg, who told us about the heroic deeds of Piet Hein and De Ruiter, about Tromp and Evertsen and Banckert.[47] We black children in the rearmost desks (the front desks were reserved for the sons and daughters of Europeans) tortured our heads by trying to cram them full of the dates of the noble houses of Holland, Bavaria, and Burgundy. We, who were caned whenever we dared to speak our own "Surinamese language" within the school walls, were expected to go into raptures about the rebelliousness of Claudius Civilis and the brave Abjuration of William the Silent.[48] We, who searched our history books in vain for the names of the rebels Boni, Baron, Joli Coeur, did our utmost so that, when the exam came, we could quickly and accurately rattle off the names and dates of the Dutch governors under whose administrations our fathers had been imported as slaves.[49]

And the system worked.

No better way to foster a sense of inferiority in a race than through this form of historical education, in which the sons of a different people are the only ones mentioned or praised. It took a long time before I could free myself entirely from the obsessive belief that a Negro is always and unreservedly inferior to any white.

I remember that one of my friends had a little sister who did not want to walk outdoors with her own brother, because his skin color was one shade darker than hers.

I remember how proud we were as little boys when white schoolmates condescended to beat us at marbles – the same European boys who felt too high and mighty to ever allow us into their homes. And we thought it was fair! That's how deeply that schoolbook history had stamped us with inferiority.

No people can reach full maturity as long as it remains burdened with an inherited sense of inferiority. That is why this book endeavors to rouse the self-respect of the Surinamese people and also to demonstrate the falsehood of the claim that the Dutch had peaceful intentions in the days of slavery.

The Pax Romana.

It has always been the excuse for every kind of imperialism.

When Ramsay MacDonald's airplanes dropped their deadly bombs on villages in the interior, it was only to preserve the Pax Britannica under which the peoples of the East could live in peace and tranquility.

In this light, even Van Heutsz is an apostle of peace.[50] And we learned to revere the long series of colonial governors as men who used the sword of peace to enforce order and security in our country, the Pax Hollandica.

If we now briefly run down the roll of governors once more, it is to show that the Pax Hollandica was nothing but the repeated crushing of desperate resistance, which kept flaring up again and again.

Van Aerssen van Sommelsdijck (1683–1688)

Let us begin with one of Holland's noblest scions, Cornelis van Aerssen van Sommelsdijck, who became the governor of Suriname on November 24, 1683. His grandfather was the well-known Baron François van Aerssen, for many years the Dutch Republic's diplomatic representative to the courts of Henry IV and Louis XIII. Cornelis grew up in the court of William II as the playmate to the Child of State and soon rose to high-ranking positions in the army.[51] As the colonel of a cavalry regiment, he fought the French invasion in 1672. He was unbending in his faith, one of those typical Calvinists who gaze out at us from old paintings, strict and righteous, over their lace collars. It is no wonder Holland was proud of this colonial governor, under whom the number of plantations increased from fifty to two hundred in only a few years and sugar production rose from three million Amsterdam pounds to seven million.[52] He flung the land of the Surinamese wide open to energetic foreigners from all the states of Europe. French réfugiés flooded in, and he gave them not only land but also the slaves needed to work it. Many of them soon achieved great wealth through trade and agriculture or rose to the colony's highest offices.

The Jews also became prosperous under Van Sommelsdijck. Samuel Nassy gave the Sephardic Jewish people a vast expanse of land later known as "Jew Savanna," which soon flourished and became the hub of Jewish life.[53] Under Scharphuizen's regime, this possession was expanded further with a gift of one hundred acres in the name of Holland.[54] Such generosity to foreigners still particularly impresses us, the Surinamese, because we hold it up against the later attitude toward the so-called liberated Negroes at the time of emancipation, which is the same attitude taken toward the country's own children today.

Yet the governors' generosity extended to other religions as well. In 1684, a number of Labadists led by Robijn settled in Suriname.[55] This group included three of the governor's sisters, a fact which may explain why they were permitted to found the beautiful plantation of La Providence. What became of these sheep and their shepherds, who set out to restore Christ's ancient flock in this fertile tropical land? To what extent did they manage to live by their principles of self-denial, the abolition of personal property, and self-sufficiency through daily labor by the members of the community? Quack tells us only that "this enterprise made little progress." What Quack neglects to tell us is that these people thought they could reconcile their religious socialist community with the ownership and exploitation of an army of slaves. The objective of all their efforts and exertions, Quack says, was complete submission to and repose in God. Well, the path they seem to have found to that destination lay in such cruel and barbaric treatment of their slaves that, as Wolbers notes, they "antagonized many people." Attacked time after time by the embittered Indians and runaway slaves, divided among themselves and exposed to all sorts of diseases, they had no choice in the end but to abandon their stronghold.

But let us return to Van Sommelsdijck.

Under his regime, the slaves slogged and sweated away.

Production rose.

Trade flourished.

Calvinist morals reigned victorious. Marriage between whites and blacks was strictly forbidden; keeping a colored mistress was the limit of what was considered tolerable. For don't the historians tell us that even the governor had taken an Indian woman for himself? And in the meantime, alongside all his everyday cares, he still found time to maintain the Pax Hollandica.

Under Van Sommelsdijck, the last vestiges of resistance among the indigenous Indians were stamped out. They put up especially fierce opposition to the incursions of the Jews, who drove them from the higher lands along the Suriname so that they could build plantations there.

To protect himself from their raids, Van Sommelsdijck first had two forts erected, one on the Commewijne River and the other along Para Creek.

In his first campaign, he destroyed five villages on the east bank of the Coppename but failed to capture their inhabitants, who fled into the wilderness.

In his second campaign, he returned to the Coppename by sea with three vessels and penetrated the interior. This time many Surinamese people were murdered or taken captive. The villages were burned down, and the Indians discovered they were no match for the white men's weapons. In this manner, Van Sommelsdijck finally forced a peace settlement with the Carib, Arawak, and Coppename peoples, in which they agreed to end their raids and were recognized by the governor as free men who would not be enslaved.

Akuba Adyosi O, Adyosi
M'uma, no krey mi gudu
na feti mi o feti
te mi fon den
mi sa kon baka

[Farewell, farewell, Acuba,
Do not weep, my wife, my darling.
To fight I go, and to struggle.
Not until victory comes
shall I return.]

This is an old, old song that I heard sung in my childhood to the accompaniment of the raison.[56] I have always imagined it stemmed from the days when these Surinamese peoples fought the Dutch. The name of the poet is no more known to us today than the names of the forefathers who left their "Acubas" to fight for freedom. At school, we learned only the names of their oppressors.

At Van Sommelsdijck's request, the States of Holland decided in 1684, in consultation with the Chartered Society, to banish convicted criminals, known as Rasphuis villains, to Suriname.[57] There they were to perform the less demanding work, because after all, even a Rasphuis villain remains superior to the Negro slaves for whom the heavy work was still reserved. This experiment in turning Suriname into a Dutch Cayenne led to a grim end for the governor. The mood among the ex-convicts soon turned mutinous. On July 19, 1688, as the governor was strolling down Oranjelaan with the commander, Laurens Verboom, he was suddenly stopped by eleven mutineers with firearms. They demanded more rations and less work. Van Sommelsdijck swiftly drew his sword, but as he raised his arm, the guns fired. The governor was dead in an instant. Verboom, hit by several bullets, died a few days later.

Three of the rebels were broken on the wheel, eight hanged, and the others sent back to Holland.

Van Sommelsdijck's son turned down the opportunity to succeed his father, and his widow sold her share in the colony to the city of Amsterdam for seven hundred thousand guilders.

In early 1689, Johan van Scharphuizen took over the colonial administration. Under his regime, a French attack with a fleet of nine ships, commanded by Jean Baptiste du Casse, was repelled by the Dutch.

In 1696, he was succeeded by Paulus van der Veen. During this administration, which went on until 1707, the whites were free to amass wealth without opposition. A strictly enforced law stated that a slave was to be regarded, deemed, and classified as personal property and a movable asset. The Surinamese came up with a proverb, "Kakalaka no abi leti na fowru mofo." (The cockroach cannot assert its rights in the bird's beak.)

The Brutes

In the decrees of the colonial governors, in the ever-stricter orders of the Governing Council, in the letters from the directors in Amsterdam, we find, time and again, with monotonous regularity and with undertones of both cruel bitterness and poorly concealed fear, the word "brutes."

The repetition of this word is so constant and so insistent in the writings of the colonial authorities that it seems almost as if all the governor's intelligence, all the soldiers' courage, and yes, the whole work of European civilization was directed at one sole aim: wiping out "the brutes" in the interior.

"The brutes" – the phrase included those of our fathers who, despite chains and guards, escaped plantation slavery; the rebels who defied the gruesome punishments and threats of the whites; the insurgents who braved the perils of the primeval forest to find, at the end of their difficult journey, death or freedom.

"The maroons" were those who flouted the law forbidding all slaves to travel by boat upriver or down; those who found the hidden routes through marshes and savannas; those who refused to be scared off when the justice authorities threatened that the punishment for any fugitive would be the severing of the Achilles tendon, the amputation of one or both legs, or death on the breaking wheel. The maroons were the uncivilized blacks, not schooled in the art of war, the men without money or weapons, against whom the stronghold of Nieuw Amsterdam was built in 1734 at the confluence of the Suriname and Commewijne rivers. And when the slave-holders' cruelty became intolerable, the maroons were the bloody avengers.

"The brutes" were those expelled from the protection of the law and hunted down by expedition after expedition, those whose villages were burned, who had a price on their heads of five guilders in 1685, rising to one hundred pounds of sugar two years later. In 1698, the reward for capturing a slave in or around Paramaribo or along the rivers was twenty-five guilders; outside those areas or along the coast, fifty guilders.

In 1717, a bounty of six hundred to fifteen hundred guilders was offered for discovering the leaders' villages and ten guilders for every villager – man, woman, or child – taken prisoner on these expeditions.

Later, a reward was promised to every European who discovered one or more villages so that they could be attacked by troops: five hundred, one thousand, or fifteen hundred guilders, depending on the degree of devastation.[58] And any slave who did not reveal everything he knew about the hiding places of the maroons was subject to the same punishments as the refugees themselves. This shows how feared, how loathed, how persecuted those maroons were; and in spite of it all, their numbers grew fast.[59] Let us examine the facts in order to learn the character of these persecuted people and that of their followers.

During the administration of Johan de Goyer (1710–1715), the French government sent two ships commanded by Admiral Jacques Cassard to Suriname. On June 8, 1712, they entered the Suriname river. Resistance from the white population forced the enemy back out to sea two days later.

But, in October of that year, Cassard returned with eight warships and approximately thirty smaller vessels. The French began to shoot at Paramaribo, went ashore at many plantations, and were soon in control of the Para and Suriname Rivers.

Since most of the European men had gone to Paramaribo to defend the forts, their white wives and children fled both the city and the plantations into the forests. They trusted more in the magnanimity of the maroons than in that of their white enemies. And their trust was not betrayed. Outside their fortifications, in defenseless bands, at the mercy of the "bush Negroes," and often weighed down with a long record of cruel treatment of their slaves, these white women and children nonetheless survived the whole episode without a scratch. Yes, it was the maroons, after the French departed on December 12, who pointed many of these whites back to the city and the plantations. It was not the maroon way to take vengeance on helpless enemies. So, may we, perhaps, in recollection of those days, demand for our black forefathers the much-abused term "civilization"?

And now the other side of the coin.

Admiral Cassard was not forced into retreat by the military achievements of the Dutch. He threatened to shoot all the plantations along the rivers to rubble if the colonial regime did not agree to his price. The administration gave in to this demand and paid Cassard three-quarters of a million guilders in bills of exchange, sugar, gold, silver, and … slaves (Indians and Negroes).[60]

And the game went on.

Back in their homes, the colonists tried first of all to reinstate the system of slavery and exploitation in all its former severity, and if possible even to intensify it to make up for their losses.

Then each planter, exhibiting the shared mentality of those days, tried to evade payment of his own share in the collective loss. Each white resident of the colony had been ordered to pay eight to ten percent of the value of his property as a contribution to the payment to Cassard. Many refused, arguing that Cassard's attack would have been repelled if the government had done more to defend the colony. Others even went so far as to send their slaves out into the forests so that they would seem poorer than they really were. Of course, they expected these slaves to return after the officials had finished taking an inventory of their property and departed. But many of these schemers saw their plan turn against them; the slaves did not return, and since many others had taken advantage of the prevailing anarchy to flee, the result of this brief period of French rule was a large increase in the number of maroons.

This loss had to be recouped, and it fell to the noble West India Company to mobilize all its forces for that purpose. The WIC, which had assumed the obligation under its 1682 charter to import as many slaves as "will be required," had also undertaken under its new charter of 1730 to supply the colony with at least twenty-five hundred slaves a year. But the African interior had by then been plundered and looted so bare that it was harder and harder to meet this obligation. So when, between 1731 and 1738, only 13,000 people were delivered instead of the 17,500 demanded, the colonists' indignation reached such heights that the Chartered Society had no choice but to send more than seventy ships to the Guinea coast to meet the demand.[61]

Time after time, the joyful gun salute was heard at Fort Zeelandia, under the proud orange, white, and blue of the old Dutch flag, as yet another ship full of slaves sailed up the Suriname River. Time after time, the white planters could hardly contain themselves until the cargo had been unloaded, inspected, and branded (at the WIC trading post's expense). Time after time, the supply of black slaves was so plentiful that the depots proved inadequate and the colonial administration had to provide a kind of "entrepôt" where the slaves could be temporarily accommodated and provided for at the price of five cents a day. Yet the great reservoir of slavery proved to be a Danaid tub[62] – not only because the overworked and exhausted slaves fell prey to large-scale epidemics and many of them contracted leprosy (an illness affecting mainly peoples living in slavery or under wretched conditions), and not only because they died of heartache and under the blows of their masters, but above all because more and more of them found their way to their liberated comrades in the forest.

The Forest Expeditions

White rule over the colony in those days was anything but a model of brotherly unity. Far better to see it as a struggle for power, waged by the most hateful and mean-spirited methods, between the governors (imported from the motherland) and the Governing Council, which was made up of twenty white colonists and had to be consulted about all matters of significance.

The two parties agreed that the maroons had to be eradicated, but the governors favored military expeditions, which would give them the opportunity to win military renown, while the Councils preferred a more cost-effective approach: trusting in the cruelty and malice of most planters, they advocated what were known as forest expeditions, which were organized by the colonists themselves and became increasingly common over time.

A case in point is the expedition led by Ensign Molinay in 1711 against the maroons in Upper Suriname. This expedition quite soon discovered one of the rebel Negro camps. They tried to catch the maroons by surprise as they slept, but their plan was foiled by the rebels' vigilance. The only slaves they captured were the two women Flora and Séry and Séry's child Patienta.

It is impossible to imagine human creatures more helpless and desolate than those three: Séry, her daughter Patienta, and Flora. The child's distress mingled in her mother's thoughts with the overpowering sense of everything she would have to go through herself. This was compounded by the loss of their all-too-brief liberty and their removal from the place where she and her child had, for a short while, lived happily. All that lay ahead for her was a ruined wasteland; her whole life had been demolished.

Even more than all this, what Séry felt was maternal love, whipped up by impending danger to a frenzy bordering on insanity. Her child was still so young, and the mere thought that soon coarse white hands would wrest her Patienta from her arms made her shudder. Shooting terrified looks at the band of white soldiers, she squeezed her daughter to her chest with convulsive force.

Every step that the white commander Molinay took toward her made her shiver. She was trembling like a leaf, blood surging to her heart. But Séry was a brave woman. She pressed her child's soft arms to her throat and kissed her again as little Patienta was torn from her embrace.

No scream came from her lips; she simply gazed at Ensign Molinay with fire in her eyes and then rose to her feet, displaying her pride to the white soldiers, defying them all without the slightest fear. She herself was surprised at the strength she seemed to have been granted, for she knew that now that her daughter was in the hands of the soldiers, the child no longer had anyone to look after her. Yet in spite of all this, she was fearless. Some force seemed to have dispelled every last twinge of fear. The weak woman had become a heroine. It was as if currents of strength were coursing through her body.

After a while, the gang of rough soldiers grabbed Séry, tied her up hand and foot, flung the poor woman to the ground, and began to thrash her with sharp sticks, in the hope that she would betray her fellows-in-misfortune. After this bloody beating, Séry seemed half-dead. The whites tried to interrogate her even in that state but could not get anything out of her. In their rage, they went at poor Séry with fire and tongs. Despite all these torments, which almost went beyond a woman's endurance, she still stubbornly refused to betray her brothers and sisters.

Her friend Flora was every bit as steadfast. Séry was forced to look on as they murdered and beheaded her.

In the words of the report:

We proceeded to the examination of the captured Negress Flora in order to discover, if possible, whether those Negroes had any other hiding place or were in communication with fugitive Negroes or Negroes from any plantation, as well as their number, the identity of their masters, and how long ago they had left, and to obtain further information about the whole nature of the business and their way of life, but *notwithstanding all the torments with fire and blows, we were never able to compel her to answer, for notwithstanding all this she remained as stubborn as ever, and by pointing at the sky, grasping a long lock of hair on her head, slapping her mouth with her fingers, and running her hand over her throat, she let us know she would rather have her head cut off than disclose any information, whether by speaking or by pointing the way.* Considering this Flora's stubbornness, we resolved to take her to Paramaribo, but we could not move her, no matter how hard we tried to make her walk or even just stand up. Having wasted a good deal of time on this and still having no means of taking her with us – for considering the mountains, creeks, and other inconveniences en route, we could not carry her, and that had been the last remaining means by which, if she had cooperated, we might have brought her with us – *we were necessitated to have her shot dead and her head chopped off, as consequently occurred forthwith.* And even if the Negress Séry had been willing enough to go with us, it so happened that her serious wound – she had been shot clean through with an arrow and her massive blood loss showed no sign of healing – made that completely impossible, thus *compelling us to have her head chopped off as well and to bring the two heads with us, as consequently occurred.*[63]

When in the days of Cassard's incursion, defenseless white women had been in the hands of the supposedly uncivilized "bush Negroes" – then they had had nothing to fear from those blacks.

But now, defenseless Surinamese women fell into the hands of supposedly civilized Dutchmen who murdered them.

Brave Séry. Brave Flora. We will always commemorate and honor your names.

1712–1742

Governors came and went in Suriname, but slavery persisted. The colony was fast becoming more prosperous. The number of plantations rose to more than four hundred. The main crop was sugar, but others began to be planted as well, such as coffee, cotton, and tobacco. In 1724 the first Surinamese coffee was auctioned in Amsterdam, in 1735 the first cotton.

The import of slaves also became big business, as we have already explained. A large number of slave scandals took place in this period. But the crueler the masters became, the greater the number of slaves who preferred the perilous escape into the forest to the inhuman demands of plantation life. The maroons thus rapidly grew in number and were increasingly on the attack in their efforts to liberate their black brothers and sisters.

The acts of the rebellious maroons in those days remind us of a fable from our fatherland: the tale of Anansi the Spider, who, seated on King Tiger's back, drove his enemy into a rage with his small but venomous bites. The rebels did not stop at a few raids but built forts in the woods, which repeatedly proved unassailable. A well-organized system of outposts kept them informed of the Europeans' movements. Furthermore, the slaves brought along by the whites on their expeditions as porters became familiar with the forest paths and used this knowledge to join the rebels.

By this stage, the company directors in Holland were making ever more insistent demands for severe measures against the fugitive slaves. This led to the decision to dispatch a force of around one hundred soldiers, led by Swallenberg, who did manage to discover three rebel villages. Around these villages he found gardens used by the maroons to grow their own food, as well as two new plots intended for the slaves from the two plantations when they joined them. Proof positive of the so-called heartlessness, laziness, and carelessness of the Negroes! Swallenberg and his soldiers caught the rebels by surprise, killed ten of them, and took two men, five women, and eleven children captive. In keeping with the time-tested methods of warfare then in use, they destroyed the gardens and razed the houses to the ground!

Hundreds of maroons were taken captive by the whites in raids of this kind and sentenced to death by the Governing Council.

Johan Jacob Mauricius (1742–1751)

Once again, a great Dutchman arrived to take over the leadership of the colony. Governor G. van der Schepper was followed by Mauricius, who had held many influential positions in the mother country. He was a pious man with such strong Christian principles that his first act as governor was to prohibit casual swearing, cursing, and desecration of God's name throughout the colony. Did Minister Donner discover this old law against profanity in the yellowed archives?[64] In any case, it shows yet again that there is nothing new under the sun.

Like Van Sommelsdijck, Mauricius was also an advocate of immigration by foreign colonists. Many farmers from the German Palatinate region and families from Switzerland came to Suriname at the governor's invitation. They were supported by the Dutch colonial administration in every possible way, but serious illnesses, maroon attacks, and a debauched way of life led most of them to their doom.

Divide and Conquer

Mauricius's greatest accomplishment was to introduce a new tactic against the maroons, based on the famous principle *divide et impera*, divide and conquer. The basic idea was to deliver a decisive blow to the rebels and destroy their villages entirely. Amid the resulting confusion, the colonists would attempt to make peace with some of them and then attack the other maroons with their new allies. Above all, he hoped to prevent the different tribes of rebels from uniting. That inspired his plan to recognize some of them as free and independent, and even to make all sorts of concessions to them, the better to persecute mercilessly those excluded from this peace treaty.

Van Sommelsdijck had already concluded a similar treaty with the Indians, and in 1739 the English had made an agreement along the same lines with some of the Jamaican rebels. Of course, Mauricius ran into opposition from the white hardliners, who were known as the cabal. For one thing, their pride would not permit them even to contemplate a treaty with the maroons; for another, they feared it would amount to acknowledging the weakness of the whites and therefore provoke still greater resistance from the rebels.

But Mauricius persisted, becoming the first to try to make peace with the rebels in the west of Saramacca.

Adu the Unbending

For some time, Mauricius had been trying to win support among the maroons for what he called his "convention." With the craftiness that marks a born ruler, he managed to use one of the sons of our country as an instrument to win the trust of the blacks. This was his slave Kwasi, who often served as a go-between. Kwasi knew the secrets of all kinds of medicinal herbs, with which he made medicines to heal the sick even after the physicians had given up on them.

On September 20, 1749, Captain Carl Otto Creutz left with his army for western Saramacca. With the greatest possible show of bravado, he tried to intimidate the maroons. They were threatened with death and utter extermination if they refused to accept the convention he had brought them. This convention had eleven articles establishing the independence of the town, as well as several provisions guaranteeing a limited freedom to trade with the whites.[65] It also, however, imposed an obligation on the rebels to hand over the slaves who had fled in 1749, as well as any who joined them later, in return for a reward of fifty guilders for each slave surrendered to the whites.

To emphasize the point, Creutz took the preliminary measure of annihilating four villages of uncooperative maroons.

Meanwhile the captain sent a few guides to the other villages to assess the mood with regard to a future treaty. One of these guides did return with soil, a bow, and arrows, symbolizing an armistice.

This was soon followed by negotiations between Captain Creutz and Adu, the chief of the Saramacca maroons: a scene worthy to be painted, turned into a print, and hung on the walls of Dutch schoolrooms. On one side is Captain Creutz, offering the chief a cane with a silver handle and promising him many more gifts from the administration the following year, to mark the definitive conclusion of the peace treaty, if he will point the whites to the dwellings of the Acouriers and Longos. On the other side is the Negro, uncivilized but also unafraid, courteously accepting the gift and reciprocating with a bow and arrows, but also politely explaining that he will cease the hostilities *but would not dream of betraying the two tribes who are his brothers and sisters, or of consenting to their destruction!*[66]

The plan was first to enter into a convention with Adu's people and then to move jointly against the tribes in Lower Samaracca and Upper Suriname. Earlier efforts had been made to discover those villages, but they had proved inaccessible, and hundreds of whites had died in the attempt in the surrounding swamps. This time the colonists had hoped that with the help of Adu's people they could attack the rebels from both sides, and now their plans were being frustrated again by the stubbornness of a "rotten Negro" who refused to act against his fellow tribes. No wonder the colonists felt little enthusiasm about concluding the peace treaty with Adu. A number of Dutchmen refused to ratify it and, as a result, almost nothing was accomplished. A few whites were sent to hand over the gifts to Adu, but when this group was waylaid and robbed of the gifts, Chief Adu, hearing nothing more from the whites, thought they had merely been trying to appease him with fair words and fine promises until reinforcements arrived from the Netherlands. Dismissing the treaty as null and void, he took up arms again.

Mauricius the Crusader

Let us leave the blood-soaked battlefield for a moment to consider the cultural measures the governor had meanwhile been trying to introduce in the colony. Under Mauricius, a plan was made to begin Christianizing the slaves. At this point, attentive readers may be rubbing their eyes in bewilderment and asking, "What are you saying? Isn't the only possible defense of slavery within Christianity that it affords a means of converting the poor heathens to the true faith? So how could it be that the Dutch lived in Suriname for more than a century before they took up missionary work in earnest?"

How are we to respond? The Dutch lack the exaggerated fanaticism of the Spanish, who showed their conquered peoples not only the blades of their swords but also Christ's cross engraved on the upper side. The Dutch are practical-minded merchants. If slaves pray, they'll have less time to work – that's all there is to it. If slaves read the Bible, they may start thinking, and slaves who think are dangerous. Thus far, the colony had got along perfectly well with two pastors, who prayed exclusively to the God of the whites for the welfare of the white community.

Mauricius, however, may have believed that Christianity, with its doctrine of salvation, might make an excellent remedy for the rebelliousness of those who might otherwise demand the benefits of salvation while still here on earth. He asked and received permission from his higher-ups in Holland to give religious education to the slaves. They even advised him to begin with slaves owned by the Chartered Company. The colonists were highly resistant to carrying out this plan, however, and Mauricius was eventually dissuaded from it by the argument that it would cost too much money. Instead, the Purmerend Redoubt was built to prevent the enemy from traveling upriver. Negroes would never be actively taught religion until after slavery was abolished.[67]

In the meantime, the whites were shocked by the revolt at Tempati Creek, where the slaves on a timber estate rose up against the director, Bruyère, when he tried to lend them to his neighbor, who was always short-handed because the slaves under his management died like rats. Bruyère knew the slaves would not wish to work for this new master, but he believed he could easily force them to do so. He said he could single-handedly tie up six slaves, throw them in a ferryboat, and bring them across. But, instead of actually demonstrating this feat of strength, he requisitioned a few burly Dutch soldiers from the colonial administration.

They showed up promptly and were supplied with enough rope to tie up uncooperative Negroes if necessary.

But the transportation of those beasts of burden did not go as smoothly as anticipated. In the ensuing slave revolt, the braggart Bruyère had both his hands cut off, two soldiers died, and more than two hundred slaves joined the Negro rebels in the forests.

Alabi

In western Marowijne and along Jouka Creek, there were many other rebel villages. Each village had its own independent leader, without any central government, but the moral authority of Chief Alabi was generally acknowledged. Although these Negroes lived in complete freedom, they did not for one moment forget the sorrowful plight of their brothers and sisters on the plantations and in Paramaribo. The attacks on white settlements by these rebel forces were no ordinary raids, as shown by the fact that before leaving the plantations they always scattered a few pamphlets written in English by a man named Boston, which made a rousing appeal for the liberation of the slaves and leveled severe threats at any white who assaulted a colored person. For each murdered Negro, the rebels promised to execute three or four whites.

The whites, having learned from experience, decided they would have to seek a settlement, negotiating with Alabi and trying to make peace with him. As usual, letters and gifts were sent to pave the way.

Then came the negotiations, which we mention mainly so that we can quote the magnificent words spoken by one of our forefathers. He was merely an ordinary Negro captain, a maroon, his body barely covered by a ragged pair of trousers or a scrap of loincloth, facing officers whose uniforms gleamed with gold thread, but they were soldiers of the colonial power and he was a son of the free woods.

Let us listen to the language of a Negro from the primeval forest.

He called it the worst of scandals for a civilized nation, such as that to which the bakras pride themselves in belonging, to consent to the abuse and torture of slaves.

> We would like to inform Your Governor and Councilors that if they wish the revolt to end, they will have to ensure that the Planters provide better treatment to the people who are their property, instead of letting them suffer abuse by Supervisors and Overseers who drink to excess, cruelly punish the Negroes, ravish their wives and daughters, neglect the ill, and thus drive large numbers of strong, hard-working people into the woods, the very people who provide for you, without whom the Colony could not survive, and whom you at long last have the undeserved good fortune of begging for peace.[68]

Thus spake the best and most enlightened of these leaders, but not all were so steadfast. In the vast expanses of the forest, the maroons were often too isolated from each other to feel solidarity, and a few tribes had grown tired of endless war and craved the peace now offered to them. In such cases Mauricius's divide-and-conquer policy was successful, and the colonial regime could eventually boast treaties with sixteen tribal chiefs. The whites and the blacks would each let a few drops of blood flow from a cut in their arm into a krabasi filled with pure spring water mixed with a little dry soil. A few drops were poured onto the ground in libation, and then everyone present had to drink from the wooden dish. The gadoman (priest) cursed all who would break the sacred covenant, and the people responded with a solemn, "Da so [So be it]."

And now?

The wilderness is still home to the free Ndyukas, the descendants of the maroons who fought for the salvation of their brothers and sisters. Their independence is acknowledged by the Dutch government. Even when a scientific expedition enters the interior, they must first politely request permission from the Negro captains. The small, self-governing communities of maroons remain untouched by the runaway desires of Duhamel's future world.[69] There discipline reigns; there order and justice are found. There are still folk days, folk songs, folk art, folkways, and the natural folklore still flourishes that Europeans are now trying to revive as a carnival attraction for foreign tourists.[70] People work in the fields and in the woods, but not without pause, and no longer than necessary to meet their simple, natural human needs.

The whites call that laziness. The Ndyuka cannot be used as a coolie on the plantations or a worker in the factories. If he needs a few products from the so-called civilized world, he glides downstream to the coastal region and offers his services for a short while for river transportation. He knows his trade but charges a high price for his services. Without any collective agreement or written employment contract, all Ndyukas have a fixed rate, and it would never occur to them to compete with each other or undercut the market. If a customer tries to insist on a lower rate, the vessel either simply stays put or else suffers an unfortunate shipwreck at the first rapids. The whites call this shameless insolence. But the Ndyuka is not yet a slave to the products of Western factories, and he knows the price of his freedom – the freedom that he, protected by treaty, enjoys in peace and security.

But what was that price?

His peace came at the cost of voluntary isolation from the rest of the world and prevents any ascent to a higher civilization or a better form of international society.

His peace came at the cost of permanent departure from the original aim of the maroons, who prepared their fields to welcome all their brothers and sisters, whom they wanted to liberate collectively from the yoke of slavery.

His peace came at the cost of a divide within the black population of Suriname.

Yes, Mauricius's divide-and-conquer policy bore fruit and created a division that will be hard to bridge.

When, in our childhood, my father came home from the gold-diggers' camp, he often brought Ndyuka friends with him, and Ndyukas later stayed at our farm when they visited the city. We children looked up to them with a kind of uneasy curiosity, as if they were wild beasts that might do anything at any moment. When they spoke, we did not understand their language. At school, we told the exciting news that Ndyukas had visited our home and made fun of their stupidity. We felt far superior to the "bush Negroes," because we had learned the noble art of reading and writing and dressed like Europeans. Yet later our only use for that noble art of writing was for signing our names in the despised livrets of the Balata Compagnieën Suriname en Guyana, in which the worker De Kom or Bidoeu or Lichtveld degraded himself to number x of series y. But in our European clothes, we were often unwittingly like prize pupils aping the schoolmaster. And the Westerns in the cinema, the fool's-gold satisfactions of the city, were often merely a cheap surrogate for the eternal beauty of the free nature in which the detested Ndyukas lived. And our very detestation was one of the tightest links in the chain binding us to the Western system of production.

Not until the old slave mentality has vanished from our hearts will the people of Suriname achieve human dignity.

Governor Crommelin (1752–1768)

Under this administrator, many of the above-mentioned atrocities against the slaves took place, and meanwhile the WIC's books recorded steep profits.

It was in this period that the colonial authorities ordained that slaves could no longer be sold privately, but only at auction. It was also in this period that more and more plantation owners entrusted others with the management of their "securities." This governor is best known, however, for carrying through the policies introduced by Mauricius and, as the Winkler Prins encyclopedia puts it, for "buying peace from the bush Negroes."

The truth of the matter is that as early as October 1760, a provisional peace treaty was signed by Alabi, Pomo, and fourteen other rebel chiefs with the colonial government as represented by Major Meyer. The main thrust of this draft treaty was that these maroons would be recognized as free people and allowed to choose their own dwelling places, as long as they kept their distance from the plantations. The treaty also promised them annual gifts from the government, in return for which they would be obliged to hand over any fugitive slaves who sought refuge with them. But when the governor, in a plenary session of the Governing Council open to the public, reported on the agreement that had been concluded, he was also required by these maroons to issue the following warning: "that the Negroes will remain true to their word once given, but that, should some slave or other come to them seeking refuge, driven to that act by his master's cruel assaults, they will never yield up that slave, because they are unwilling to surrender their tortured brothers, after the agonies they have already endured, back into the cruel hands of the colonial government."[71]

Furthermore, the peace was still far from complete, since many rebellious chiefs, including the great "Zamzam" of the Upper Saramaka, resisted every form of peace with the whites. The treaties entailed no more than an armistice. One cannot imagine a clearer testimony to the intentions of the maroons than the fact that their struggle and their rebel spirit endured for as long as slavery remained lawful on Surinamese soil!

Governor Nepveu (1770–1779)

The Winkler Prins encyclopedia offers this very dry remark about Crommelin's peace treaties: "They did not lead to the return of peace at all, and in fact, a formidable slave revolt ensued in 1772." This covers the entire term as governor of Jan Nepveu, the former public prosecutor, a time when it seemed the white regime might collapse once and for all as it was hammered ever harder by the rebels. And what of the attacks, first on the plantations of the cruelest oppressors, and later, systematically and strategically, on Dutch military posts as well? The Cottica confederation? Nothing and nothing. Not one word about Boni, not one letter about Baron, not one sentence about Joli Coeur – those heroic maroon chiefs. This is how a standard Dutch reference book informs its readers about the history of a Dutch colony. "In 1778, after the slaves had finally been subdued completely, an era of peace and prosperity dawned." Whose peace? Whose prosperity? And how much blood did it cost, how much cruelty, how much destruction?!

Buku (Decayed into Dust)

Baron

The Negro Baron had been the slave of the Swede Carel Gustaf Dahlberg, one of the many foreigners who quickly amassed great stores of treasure in Suriname. Ever since his early childhood, this young black man had stood out for his intelligence, which was so exceptional that his master thought it would be useful to have him schooled in the art of reading and writing (as colored people almost never were). His master also allowed him to learn a trade and later took him on a trip to Holland.

What a wondrous world opened up to that gifted young black man here! How his lively, jet-black eyes drank in the sight of a society whose people scarcely seemed to know the word "slavery." How his pulse raced when he beheld a culture in which work was done naturally and with joy, without a white officer cracking his whip over the backs of the workers. How his heart must have burned with gratitude when his master promised to grant him his freedom upon his return to Suriname. Young Baron was a slave with wings, a dreamer of great dreams, but also a realist, who could not forget the cruel sights of his childhood, and a loving brother to his companions in misery.

Maybe in some little Dutch village church, Baron heard the pastor preach about the high calling of Moses, who led his people out of slavery in Egypt. Maybe he even dreamed that he could lead his people to freedom, without bloodshed, with the help and support of noble liberal spirits such as his master, who, after all, had personally promised him his freedom.

Poor crippled dreams, poor betrayed trust in his master's word. No sooner were they back in Suriname than Dahlberg proved to have forgotten his promise and sold the young Negro to one of his friends, who deemed it necessary to teach this rebellious spirit the basic principles of slavery all over again by subjecting him to the "Spanish billy goat" on the scaffold.

Yet the young hero of liberty was too resilient to be broken by his master's whip. He left the plantations one night and soon became one of the most distinguished leaders of the rebel troops. Thanks to his great energy, he gathered together the scattered rebels to attack the white colonists from the stronghold he had founded, the fort given the proud name of "Buku" – "decayed into dust" – as a sign that he and his men would rather decay into dust then surrender it to the whites.

The Chieftain Joli Coeur

The Negro Joli Coeur had also been a slave, with the misfortune to be born on Rodebank Plantation. This plantation was in the grip of the Dutchman Schulz, infamous for his cruel treatment of his slaves and the crude depravity to which he subjected his powerless slave women.

Although Governor Van Aerssen van Sommelsdijck, a strict Calvinist, had prohibited intermarriage between whites and Negroes as early as 1683, there was a general belief among whites that this prohibition did not apply to the nights of pleasure for which they now and then selected one of their slave women.

So it was unseemly and illegal, no doubt, that Joli Coeur's father fought tooth and claw when one night his master crept into the slave dwelling to demand Joli Coeur's mother for his bed that night.

And we may likewise conclude that the colonial justice system was mild in its judgment when it condemned the Negro to no more than a severe "Spanish billy goat" for this act of resistance. But the young Joli Coeur, who had to witness his father's punishment, felt every blow as if it were landing on his own back. He could never forget how his mother had been abused, and the whole rest of his proud life was devoted to avenging that act.

The Chieftain Boni

In his veins flowed the blood of the whites. He was not born in slavery, he never wore the chains of bondage, and no one dared brand his skin with the master's mark.

He grew up in the wilderness and understood every sign in the secret, silent language of the forest primeval.

In him the strength and courage of the jaguar were united with the slender swiftness of our deer.

But above all, his personality was marked by the same noble pride we also find in his mother.

She must have been beautiful, that young slave woman, to be chosen month after month to lie with her master.

She must have been so beautiful that a touching episode unfolded on that plantation, as if a budding romance might forge lasting bonds between the two.

Most of all, she must have been brave. When the bird of love had flown the nest and the warm spot in her white master's heart had cooled, when he raised the lash once again over the black woman who was carrying his child below her heart, she did not try to win back his lost affection with pleading or flattery, but sought out the dark and dangerous path to the ancient forest, home to her liberated comrades.

Brave little woman. Caimans swam in the rivers, the jaguar lurked in the brush, and the undergrowth concealed venomous snakes, but crueler than all the creatures of the wilderness were the panting bloodhounds the white master put on her trail.

She hid. She heard the baying of the bloodhounds searching in the distance. She dragged her pregnant body onward through the tangled snarls of tree fern and vine. She fed on wild fruit, without ever having learned on the plantation to tell the nutritious from the poisonous plants. She set her naked feet on the few patches of solid ground that formed a muddy path through the deadly peril of the swamps. She found her way to the concealed maroon camp, and she gave birth to her son Boni in liberty!

Baron, deceived and abused, and Joli Coeur, scorned and goaded, joined forces with Boni, the scourge of the whites. These chieftains brought order and discipline to the

Surinamese rebels and created a military force that held its own for centuries against the well-organized Dutch force.

The colored leaders, honored for their manly valor and beloved for their incorruptible integrity, were regarded throughout Suriname as the natural protectors of the oppressed. Rarely have chieftains exerted such a powerful influence on their followers as these maroon leaders.

Any fugitive slaves who arrived to join the rebels were put on a long probation. If they made it through this trial, they were armed and integrated into one of the rebel bands. This was how the maroons assembled a first-rate army.

Open Warfare
To combat the growing maroon threat effectively, the colonial government, acting on a proposal from Nepveu, raised a powerful army. They decided to locate the rebel leader Baron's fortified base and attack it. The encampment was very strong, attesting not only to the blacks' hard and skillful work, but also to Baron's natural aptitude for strategy.

The fort was in the middle of a vast marsh without solid ground. It was surrounded by black palisades three times the height of a man, and behind the embrasures were small cannons and swivel guns. Its name was Buku, "decayed into dust," and from its highest point flew a proud yellow banner with a black lion. The whites attempted two attacks and more, but with no success; they could not ford the marsh or breach the palisades. The attackers could not use their cannons there, and the hand grenade had not yet been invented. So, even though the Europeans stood before the rebel village with a fairly substantial army, they were utterly powerless.

The Dutch colonial government then decided to try a different tactic, offering a general amnesty to any Negroes who would lay down their arms and surrender to the whites. But Baron mocked the pretty words of the Europeans, laughing and warning his people not to accept the Dutch offer. For he had learned from bitter experience what a white man's promise was worth.

Meanwhile, twelve colored rangers or Redimusu (so-called "redeemed" slaves, bought out of slavery, who were trained and led by white officers) ventured close to the village, where they were captured by Baron's troops. When they refused to join the rebel force, eleven were shot dead and the twelfth was sent back with the message that Baron's troops feared neither the Redimusu nor the whites.

After these initial defeats, the government in Paramaribo sent Captain Mayland to fight the rebels with a strong European army, assisted by two hundred colored guides (redeemed slaves) under the command of De Friderici. When Baron saw them approaching, he defiantly planted a banner on top of his fortress, upon which both sides opened fire, but to little avail. Mayland attempted to make a path through the marsh by dropping in bundles of sticks. This too was a failure, and many whites died in these pointless endeavors. They began to run short of food and material, and the Dutch began planning to lift the siege. But then they chanced upon the secret path, covered by only a shallow layer of water, which led to a secret entrance to the fort.

Mayland immediately mounted a feint attack and, while Baron was assembling all his troops at the place under threat, De Friderici and his guides forded the marsh unnoticed and climbed the palisades unopposed.

A terrible bloodbath ensued.

"Buku" was taken.

The churches of Paramaribo held services to give thanks for this victory.

Mayland's army returned to the city with its prisoners: four men, twenty-six women, nineteen children, and the severed hands of nine revolutionaries.[72]

But Baron and Boni, who had escaped the bloodbath, assembled their scattered troops and built a new camp between the Paramaka and the Coermotibo. This time the white lieutenant Leppert was sent out with a smaller force to destroy the camp. But the rebels went out to meet their attackers, waged battle in the wilderness, and managed to kill most of them and send the others fleeing in panic. Leppert himself was struck down in this skirmish.

Soon afterwards, Baron and his reconstituted force launched a full frontal assault, raiding the plantations of Suynigheyt, Pérou, and l'Espérance and thereby settling the score for Buku with the Dutch.

We wish to attempt to shed light on Baron's character by sketching a pair of incidents from his life.

During one of these battles, he was brought the captured white officer Muller. When Baron heard that Muller had arrived from Holland not long before, he sent him back to Paramaribo unharmed with the words: "Go your way, you have not yet been in Suriname long enough to abuse our enslaved brothers and sisters." One of Baron's men had stripped Muller of his outer garments; Baron ordered that they be returned and even gave his adversary a hat to protect his head from the tropical sun and the monsoons.[73]

On another occasion, the rebels had taken white soldiers prisoner. If they had treated their prisoners the same way the whites dealt with captured maroons, then these soldiers would surely have been put to death. Instead, Baron realized that the mercenaries were not the source of the disagreements, but simply people forced to be his enemies under so-called military discipline. He protected them from the anger and hate of his followers, supplied them with food, and promptly sent them back to the city.[74]

We defy one and all to show us that whites have ever, at any time in Surinamese history, treated colored people this way!

Foreign Military Assistance
Carthage had to be destroyed, and it is the white man's task to pacify the blasted bush Negroes.

The colonial government and the white colonists, up in arms at what Baron had done, urged the Chartered Society and the States General to increase the military presence in Suriname. Our protector William V therefore sent a force of 800 men in December 1772, commanded by the Swiss officer Louis Henri Fourgeaud, to subjugate the maroons.[75]

Fourgeaud, who had earned his stripes as the bloody brute who quelled the slave rebellion in Berbice, was ordered to attack and destroy the rebels with his troops. His second-in-command for this expedition was Major Medler. They reached a vast field planted with rice and wheat. Beyond it rose the rebel base, a peaceable and prosperous village built in a circular form and sheltered from the sun by the foliage of the tall trees. As they crossed this field, the maroons started shooting, and the two sides became involved in a fierce firefight, which went on for more than an hour. The losses among the whites would doubtless have been much greater if the rebels had had lead bullets. But these were as good as absent from the arsenal of Baron's army, so instead the maroons had to make do with pieces of gravel, bits of coins, and bone buttons. No wonder they were eventually forced to retreat behind their fortifications.

The white troops came closer and closer. Before long the village would fall into their hands, and once again they would spare neither women nor children. This was the moment when one maroon leader put a torch to the huts and sheds that his people had built, setting the village aflame.

Behind the screen of smoke and flames, the rebels, while firing on their enemies, were able to transport their women and children and the most essential goods to safety. On one side, Baron's troops were protected by the impassable marshes; on the other, the advance of the whites was checked by the raging flames. It was as if all hell had burst loose. The gunfire, the cursing and roaring of the whites, and the wails of the wounded and the dying mingled with the shrill blasts of the bugles, as thick clouds of smoke and ash were whirled up in the wind and made it impossible to survey the battleground. And, meanwhile, as the men fought, the women and children were weaving large baskets and filling them with rice, cassava, and yamsi, so that they would have enough food for the days ahead.

When finally, at nightfall, the last flames began to die out, Fourgeaud understood why Baron had given the fort the intrepid name of Cosaai ("Come on!"). He no longer sought to wipe out the maroons by force but tried to enter into negotiations with them. On his own authority, he promised the maroons life, freedom, and plenty of food and drink in return for their voluntary surrender.

Then one rebel asked, "Who are you to come here and suddenly promise us all this?"

He replied, "I am the white chief Fourgeaud."

When the maroons had heard this, they replied with loud laughter, "We have nothing to say to you, you half-starved Swiss, and we have no respect for your mistress, the Dutch government, either. You whites are always generous with your promises, but you have yet to show the same talent for keeping your word. You're just like the tiger who promised not to eat the tender doe but remembered his promise only after he had devoured her."

Toward morning, when Fourgeaud was ready to resume the fighting, the maroons had vanished without a trace. In the end, the exhaustion of his troops and a shortage of rations forced him to withdraw.

Soon after these events, a large number of maroons and their chieftain Boni (Baron had died in combat) crossed the Maroni to settle on French territory. The French, disturbed by this development, sent an intendant, V.P. Malouet, to Suriname. In the most courteous terms, but no less serious for that, he informed the Dutch colonial government that the relative frequency of slave revolts in Suriname should be ascribed to two factors. The first was the failure to "rein in many masters in the mistreatment of their slaves." He described these masters as "the true inciters of the chaos in the interior," adding that the government, by tolerating their misdeeds and denying the slaves any form of protection, had betrayed a narrow-minded outlook at a time when the colony's security hung in the balance. The second factor was the lack of religious education for the slaves. The French, Malouet explained, "planned to send priests to the maroons in their territory, invited the Dutch colonial government to do the same, and would not only welcome any priests or other clergymen sent by the Dutch regime but also support them in all sorts of ways."[76]

But the Governing Council ruled that it would be preferable to "exterminate those brutes completely" and declared that its firm decision was "that if the maroons returned to Surinamese territory, they would be captured or killed."[77]

This warm invitation does not seem to have tempted the maroons. Or at least, they remained on the far bank, living in peace and a degree of comfort. The French were sensible enough to leave them be in their villages, so the maroons had no reason whatsoever to trouble the European planters in the area. There were no raids on the plantations.

For a time, the Dutch territory also benefited from this cessation of hostilities. Boni and his comrades, however, were still burning to liberate their Surinamese brothers and sisters from their bondage, and in 1788, he returned to fight once more for the freedom of Suriname's slaves.

The Final Chapter for the Resistance

In Europe, the flag of freedom was flying. Jean-Jacques Rousseau described the idyllic circumstances of peoples living in nature. The natural rights of the people and of the citizen were established. The cry of "liberty, equality, fraternity" rang out in the streets. The French sans-culottes stormed the Bastille, and the Dutch Patriots plodded after them, glancing around all the while to see if anyone disapproved. In an immense fire of enthusiasm, Paris burned the ropes that had bound the underclass. The flames rose so high that a few sparks blew all the way across the ocean to Suriname, where they set off smoky fires in the damp Dutch peat of a few white souls.

Smoldering soul-fires like these emerge from Dutch hearts as the sputtering rhymes of Catsian odes.[78] So it was that the Surinamese poet P.F. Roos presented our fatherland with an ode to freedom bearing the modest title of "Suriname extolled in doggerel." "Raise temples devoted to sacred freedom," the inspired poet sang, and a little further on he exclaimed, "O, may the day come when Africa will once again be a storehouse of sturdy slaves for the Netherlands!"[79] He illustrates the spirit of the age: "Freedom for us, slavery for you," and the great god Mammon will turn the realm of freedom and equality into a reality.

In 1780, Commander Bernard Texier succeeded the deceased governor, Jan Nepveu. It was the time of the Fourth Anglo-Dutch War, in which the Dutch lost Berbice, Demerara, St. Eustatius, and Essequibo. An English privateer plied the coast, robbing Dutch and American ships, a lucrative line of work. But was that buccaneer really an Englishman, with the distinctly un-British name of Hans Stiers? Or was he perhaps one of the Dutchmen who had declared in advance that they would sail straight through hell if there was money in it?

Oh, well, what do we care anyway? What does it matter to us that the lost Dutch possessions fell back into Dutch hands in 1784 when peace was made; or that William V instructed the new governor, De Friderici (installed on August 24, 1792), to welcome British troops as allies; or that De Friderici himself surrendered the colony without the least struggle to Lord Hugh Seymour's fleet on August 13, 1799 and, in return, was allowed to retain his position as governor? In the end, what do all these intrigues matter to us, the Surinamese, beside the one immense fact that stands out like a black silhouette against the light of the European revolution: that this was the time, just as the morning light of freedom was dawning for the whites, when in Sranan the last great wave of the struggle for liberation from slavery came crashing down.

Oh, we understand perfectly well that the government was alarmed when the occasional slave openly displayed the tricolor cockade of liberty. We can well imagine they did not intend for the rebellious maroons to follow the example of the Bastille-stormers so admired by a certain Mr. Roos.

We appreciate their horror when they heard the rumor that the great maroon leader Boni had once again unfurled the banner of revolt.

Chieftain Boni and his followers were attacked by the whites on Aroku, an island in the Maroni, a village betrayed to the whites by Boni's second-in-command Ascaan. With fierce courage, Boni's maroons threw themselves into the heat of battle, but in the end they had to yield. A large proportion of these rebel troops escaped, but their power had been broken. The maroons were scattered now, and from then on the lives of those stalwart heroes were full of misery, destitution, famine, and the bullets of the whites in constant pursuit.

The brave and powerful leader of the maroons could no longer hold his once fearsome army together, and those who had worked zealously to betray Boni were rewarded for their loyal service to the Dutch colonial regime.

When one of the last remaining bands of maroons was caught unawares, twenty of them were killed, including Boni, Kormantijn Kodjo, and Puja.

They were counted among the brutes, as the whites called the maroons in those days, but to us they are and will remain heroes of Suriname, who won their proud status as leaders through bravery and virtue, fighters for the rights and liberty of Surinamese slaves.

Baron! Boni! Joli Coeur!

Your memory will be forever cherished in our hearts. You are part of us.

Suriname under British Rule

Slaves are passed from master to master, and even a colony is no more than a passive object in the horse trades of Europe's great powers. In 1802, the Treaty of Amiens gave Holland its colonies back, with the exception of Ceylon. De Friderici's term of office came to an end, and in December of that year he retired to his plantations. The new head of the regime was Willem Otto Bloys van Treslong, succeeded in 1803 by Pierre Beranger. Then, on April 30, 1804, the British re-entered the scene. Commanded by Sir Charles Green and Sir Samuel Hood, they sailed upriver, and a few vigorous attacks on the forts were enough to force the commander, Lieutenant Colonel B.A. Batenburg, to surrender the position.[80] Soon afterwards, many colonists were relieved to learn that the British would let them go on making good money. The new governor, Sir Charles, began by reassuring them that under the British regime all Europeans would retain their freedom and the peaceful enjoyment of their possessions.

This statement was far from superfluous, because as early as De Friderici's administration, a dark shadow had fallen over the colonists' happiness. While in Dutch Suriname, atrocities like Varenhorst's and those on Arendsrust Plantation (see above) were still taking place, in the land of the revolution, immediately after the execution of Louis XVI, the National Convention decided to abolish slavery in the French colonies. And this law was no dead letter, as shown by the fact that the authorities in Paris decreed the banishment of many of Cayenne's most prominent white tyrants. This banishment gave the Netherlands the opportunity to demonstrate its commitment to the right of asylum; the slaveholders received a warm welcome from De Friderici. In a sense, their arrival confirmed De Friderici's happy expectation that Cayenne's plantation owners "would be less averse to continuing to work with slaves under Dutch protection than to seeing their possessions destroyed in the name of France and leaving them at the mercy of a lawless mob."[81]

Yet, on the other hand, growing numbers of draconian ordinances, "Spanish billy goats," and chains, as well as an army of soldiers, were needed to prevent the exodus of too many slaves to the land of liberty. So you can imagine the collective sigh of relief when robust British conservatism was found to despise the newfangled French ways. Yet even the British, who had never stood out for their sentimentality as colonial rulers anywhere in the world, were outraged by the prevailing Dutch methods and practices.

After Green, the colony had a series of three British governors: William Carlyon Hughes from 1805 to 1808, Charles Bentinck from 1809 to 1811, and Pinson Bonham from 1811 to 1815. Under Hughes, the first protests by British officers began against the practice of allowing private slaveholders to have their slaves disciplined at Fort Zeelandia. They regarded this as an affront to the British flag and demanded an end to "the cries of these poor wretches suffering torture."[82] Their petition enraged the Dutch, who considered it an insult even to refer to such treatment as torture, since it was "an integral part of the lives of the slave population." It should be added that this was a time-honored practice, that Fort Zeelandia's location was ideal for the administration of such punishments, that the Dutch were apparently unflustered in those days by the cries of fear and pain audible throughout the city, and that most of the colonists would have regarded the termination of this long-established practice as an infringement of their sacred property rights.

Still worse in their eyes was the leniency shown by the British to four mutinous riflemen taken prisoner. What the mutineers had done was without a doubt hugely significant and could have had far-reaching implications. The Dutch administration had tried, as any colonial regime would, to shift some of the burden of defending the colony to the indigenous people, offering them relative freedom, good pay, uniforms, and other privileges in exchange for turning against their own compatriots. For example, Suriname then had a corps of more than four hundred riflemen, or Redimusu, whose reliability had never yet been subject to doubt. But sooner or later blood will tell, and to the astonishment of the Europeans, two detachments of around thirty men each suddenly turned their weapons on their officers, mutinied, and joined the maroons. Even though Hughes visited the battlefield in person, he was unable to subdue the insurrectionists.

But, thanks to good fortune, betrayal, and deceit, four mutineers were taken prisoner. The Dutch colonists cried out for vengeance, demanding a sentence so horrifically cruel that the Redimusu would be cowed into obedience. The old cross and the heavy crowbar had already been fetched from storage so that the unfortunate men could be broken on the wheel, limb by limb. Imagine how much scorn the Dutch colonists heaped on Hughes when he decided – in the year 1807! – that breaking on the wheel was an outdated punishment and that the four mutineers would merely be hanged, after which their bodies were decapitated and burned.

But the colonists' outrage knew no limits when the British parliament prohibited the slave trade with effect from 1808. The annual number of imported slaves had been capped earlier, in 1806, at three percent of the number already in the colony. The result was that only 987 slaves were imported in 1806 and only 467 the following year. So, it is not surprising that the ban of 1808 was a dead letter, or that a clandestine slave trade soon developed, with an estimated 1,000 slaves smuggled into the country each year. Most Dutchmen showed as little respect for the law in those days as Americans showed for their own famous Prohibition.

Throughout this period, the actual work of administration was mostly in British hands. High positions were often even assigned to British nationals who remained in the mother country and delegated their colonial positions to others for a fee. The country was flooded with soldiers, and large numbers of newly created positions afforded young Englishmen a good living. If the costs of this administrative apparatus weighed very heavily on the indigenous people, that was simply part of the system. As for the Dutch, their councils were still opened with great pomp and circumstance, rivaling Prinsjesdag.[83] In reality, however, they had lost most or all of their influence.

On November 20, 1815, the Treaty of Paris returned all the colonies conquered by the British to the Netherlands, except for Berbice, Demerara, Essequibo, and the Cape. Suriname thus became a Dutch possession again. The new constitution gave King William I sole supreme authority over the colonies. New regulations were drawn up for the administration of Suriname, and on February 26, 1816, the English flag was lowered and the Dutch tricolor raised. It would be another half century before slavery was abolished.

The Great Fire

In the colony's upper echelons, history rolled on with the deadly monotony of a machine.[84]

> February 27, 1816, to July 9, 1816: Governor Willem Benjamin van Panhuys
> 1816 to 1822: Governor Cornelis Vaillant
> 1822 to 1827: Governor Abraham de Veer
> 1827 to 1828: Governor Johannes van den Bosch
> 1828 to 1831: Governor Paulus Roelof Cantz'laar
> 1832 to 1838: Governor Evert Ludolph, Baron van Heeckeren van Waliën

The colony is a clearing house for governors, a rung on the colonial career ladder. New leaders imported in much the same way as bales of cotton cloth from Twente. Knowledge of the people, love of the country, or attachment to the territory to be governed – all these varieties of wisdom must be gained, as far as they can be, from personal experience while in office. As far as seeing the big picture or carrying out a plan that will survive one's own term of office, there is not enough time, and no need in any case, as one is merely playing European constable among the niggers, moving one's savings into a secure strongbox, and all the while longing for the day when one can leave this accursed country.

And on the underside of the colony we find the same regularity – that of cruel and inhumane slavery – interrupted only by the resistance that kept flaring up anew. A government commission investigated the condition of the slaves' health. After all, "the slave population is commended to the special protection of the Dutch colonial administration. They will always use the most effective means, insofar as is possible without infringing on the rights of the owners or posing a threat to the peace and security of the colony, to improve the circumstances of the slaves and advance the welfare of same."

The commission determined that the health conditions of the slaves were appalling. The death rate was abnormally high. The number of slaves who had died of neglect was calculated to be about 15,000.

Yet the rights of the owners did not allow for any serious measures. The situation remained the same, just as it did after every one of the many Surinamese reports. The slaves had to go on starving and lacking the necessities of life, unless they revolted again, like the slaves in Nickerie in 1821 or the maroons who resumed their attacks on the plantations in 1829. Such revolts were decisively crushed. A new colonial charter was introduced. New taxes were imposed, more burdensome each time. And the whip lashed the slaves' backs so that the new taxes could be paid out of new profits.

Once upon a time, in the year 1832, there were two young Negroes. The older one was eighteen, the younger one fourteen. One was named Frederik, the other Kodjo. They probably stood trembling many times outside the walls of Fort Zeelandia when they heard the grievous cries of the tortured people.

They undoubtedly saw the "Spanish billy goat" administered on the street corners of Paramaribo and, like the British officers, listened to "those poor wretches suffering torture." And they themselves, enslaved since birth, must have experienced time and again how it feels when a white officer's whip lashes your black skin.

Their master had sent them into the city to hawk bread rolls in the streets. Kodjo had been paid two and a half cents too little, and Frederik had lost eight cents that same day. It was primal fear, an animal's fear of being struck, that kept them from returning to their master that evening. The next day they realized that their failure to return had put them in danger of still severer punishment. They went to live in the forest near Paramaribo and over time were joined by a few other outcasts, boys like them, in danger as they were, who had fled their masters' tyranny for one reason or another.

They lived in the forest, but these young Negroes were not plantation slaves; having grown up in the city, they felt like strangers to the wilderness and had never learned the art of feeding on its fruits and plants. They went hungry. When night fell, they went on raids for food in the outskirts of the city. They lived in constant fear of discovery. They were spotted, pursued, and sometimes had to flee back into their forest before they had even found anything to eat.

Then they came up with a plan to start a fire and, in the ensuing chaos, to steal so much money and provender that they could live free in the woods. On the evening of September 3, a fire broke out in a district of Paramaribo. Behind the stately homes of the whites, in the warren of huts and slums that then made up the capital, the ravenous flames found plenty of food. There was no capable fire brigade, no organization that could have stopped this disaster at its outset. In a few short hours, a very large part of Paramaribo fell prey to the flames.

Were the young Negroes shocked by the outcome of their acts? Was the light of the flames too bright for them to follow through on their original plan? All we know is that the price put on their heads did its work. The slaves Kodjo, Mentor, Present, and Frederik were captured a few days after the fire, and their friends soon afterwards.

The public prosecution service, under its Dutch acting director Kanter, demanded that Kodjo be hanged and his head chopped off and put on display. The sentence requested for the others was flogging and branding and some period of forced labor in chains. The Colonial Court of Justice rejected this request and, in the name of the King, condemned Kodjo, Mentor, and Present to be burned alive, Winst and Tom to be hanged, and the others clapped in chains, flogged, and forced to labor for the rest of their lives.[85]

Just a little imagination, dear reader, and you can envision what they felt in the days between the sentence and its execution. A little imagination and you can picture that packed square in Paramaribo where the smell of roasted human flesh rose into the air. This was in 1833, soon after Van Speijk, around the time of Bellamy's verses about sentimental prose.[86]

In the time when three Negro boys were burned alive, two others were hanged, and five sentenced to forced labor for life. Most of them were not yet twenty years old.

Ah, the memory of this act that we preserve in our hearts is not a pretty one!

The Fate of the Ethical

On the colonial chessboard, no move is weaker than the one inspired by ethical principles. Over the long span of the Dutch regime, the white population undoubtedly included good, progressive elements; there were undoubtedly plantation owners who tried to treat their slaves with human dignity, officials who did their duty with loyal honesty, and soldiers whose humble courage was beyond all question. Why have we overlooked them here? Not out of demagoguery, but simply because the acts of the authorities, and the many atrocities, and the public response, all show us that these better elements did not influence the general mentality. The regrettable but undeniable truth is that in the colonial system, the whole chain is no stronger than its weakest link. It may be the case that a few planters, alarmed by their slaves' poor health, decided a better diet would be advisable, one including some fat and meat. It is also possible that certain planters objected for reasons of conscience to the separate sale or hiring-out of slaves from a single household. But when the majority of colonists clearly stated through their actions that such measures were essential to the cost-effective operation of the sugar companies, the others could not remain outside this system indefinitely, lest they face economic catastrophe and the general contempt of their fellow colonists.

And what was true of private persons was still truer of the colony's governors. There is a Dutch proverb: "You can't vault higher than your pole is long." The pole with which the ethical administrator sought to vault was very short, since it was made from the costly wood of avarice. A governor like Van Heeckeren – who, if Halberstadt's account can be believed, was put on trial during Van den Bosch's term of office for the unlawful possession of field Negroes, and who exercised his power in all sorts of unjustifiable ways against foreign nationals (John Bent) – can advance his career in such a colony.[87] He is permitted to intercept private correspondence, to recruit sons to spy on their fathers, to dismiss honest officials with eighteen years of service behind them (Halberstadt) without giving them the opportunity to defend themselves, to hand out honors and decorations to his friends so brazenly that, until he was exposed, forged orders of merit were circulating in the colony. None of this troubles him; his position is unthreatened, and an honorable discharge awaits him at the end of his career. The ethical individual, in contrast, does not realize that he is often pushed forward as a buffer against the radicals, for fear of a poor reputation abroad or to prevent the mass desertion of slaves to freer colonies. If he is serious about his mission, he will soon discover that Halberstadt was right about the character of the colonists when he wrote the following about Suriname:

> In any tropical colony, the genuine colonists and free long-term residents are very few in number and have a very feeble influence on the administration. Many of them, both the private individuals and the officials, went there specifically to enrich themselves by any means possible and restore a squandered fortune, or to wallow drunkenly in tropical bounty; and without forceful action by the supreme authority to keep each person within the bounds of his duty, this overriding tendency and the feeble influence of popular opinion must needs lead to the heights of conspiracy, toadying, extortion, and swindling, with pernicious repercussions for land and property.[88]

Such a population will always oppose any truly ethical course of action with all its might. And if death had not caught up with Van Heeckeren in Curaçao, he could have enjoyed the rest of his days with an untroubled conscience, while Burchard Joan Elias, the noble figure who governed Suriname from 1842 to 1845, left the colony with a broken heart, and the idealist Reinier Frederik, Baron van Raders, a man of science and learning, was sent home with a red passport.[89]

In Conflict with Amsterdam Merchants

It was a disagreeable task, no doubt, to take over the administration of a colony from a governor who not long before had restored a person convicted of sex offenses against eighteen slave women to a public office whose duties included "helping to ensure a high degree of compliance with laws and regulations, especially with regard to the treatment of slaves"! In such a colony, there was no pleasure in taking up the task of introducing new regulations on slavery, when a reward of ten guilders had been promised for every fugitive slave shot dead, upon presentation of the severed hand as evidence.

It was impossible to carry out such a task in a place where everyone had a direct financial interest in perpetuating slavery.

The regulations on slavery then in force dated from 1782. Elias believed that for new regulations to be of any use, they would have to be enforced not by the Administrators and Directors, but by impartial officials. It was especially important to him to set limits on the punishment of house slaves. To this end he launched an investigation and, where he found what he deemed to be excessive punishment of house slaves, he sent the criminal records to the Netherlands, so that the Dutch government would be fully informed of the situation in Suriname.

The criminal records from the time (weekly reports from the deputy police lieutenant and the warden of Fort Zeelandia) often state that one hundred lashes were administered by officials in the justice system at a slaveowner's request, without any outside investigation. These officials, charged with serving Justice, earned much of their income in this way, and the emoluments increased with the number of lashes. Elias reported to the Dutch government that the number of lashes with tamarind switches had sometimes risen as high as two or three hundred before he made the bounds of house slave punishment the object of investigation, yet in petitions from Amsterdam merchants he was accused of creating barriers to essential domestic discipline.[90]

Oh, the indignation of those Amsterdam merchants, who saw any alteration of the established rules without their consent as a violation of their sacred rights of property! How solemn the sound, coming from their distinguished lips, of the declaration "that the present Governor-General, with greater passion than prudence, supports philanthropical notions, and that his conduct shows a regrettable lack of conservative principles."[91] How they protested once more, in their new petition of November 25, 1843, "against the Governor-General's violation of the jurisdiction over one's own home that is the long-established custom of the colony and without which the institution of slavery would, to some extent, be inconceivable."[92] And, meanwhile, how determined they were to undermine the said governor's authority, sparing no means, however repugnant.

Libel was one of the colony's most fearsome weapons. In earlier times, Sir Pinson Bonham had learned that lesson; he wrote to Lord Bathurst that he had been left with no choice but to bar people who had dined at his table daily from entering his house, and that Bent could report to the minister how maligned and insulted he had been.

Seldom, however, has a libel campaign showed such sophistication or involved such blatantly false figures as the one financed by the Amsterdam merchants.[93] The makers of the false document were dismissed from their positions by Royal Decree of 1844, but this provoked such outrage in the colony that the Amsterdam merchants petitioned the minister yet again and then turned to the Lower House of the Dutch parliament. In the meantime, the new regulations on slavery had to be postponed. Governor Elias, weary of all this scheming, tendered his resignation. The Amsterdam gentlemen had prevailed: soon, the plan for new regulations on slavery had been abandoned completely, and Mr. Elias left before his successor even arrived, so eager was he to put the land of libel behind him. He had experienced the consequences of pursuing an ethical policy in this Dutch colony! But the episode later had a sequel: the tragedy in which Baron van Raders was forced to play the lead.

White Settlement

Can Suriname, as large and thinly populated as it is, become a destination for the Dutch surplus population? Might the fertile soil of Sranan allow Dutch farm families to achieve prosperity through their own labors and serve as an example to the indigenous population with their superior agricultural methods?

Is this a theoretical possibility? Wolbers's answer is an emphatic yes and, in recent years, the idea of settlement by Dutch colonists has once again been vigorously defended by experts (such as the newly appointed governor, Professor Johannes Coenraad Kielstra, writing in the *Haagsche Maandblad* in 1925).

So why did past attempts fail? They failed, as every plan to bring prosperity to the colony has failed, because of conservative obstinacy among the colonial administrators themselves, because of narrow-minded, faint-hearted economies that made it impossible to obtain enough initial capital, and because of a lack of perseverance in the face of setbacks. It was Governor Elias who, foreseeing the inevitable emancipation of the slaves, set up trials of European settlement along the Saramaka. It was this same prospect that made the colony's plantation owners and their supporters oppose the plan from the outset. Already the slaves on either side of the colony had been freed, but the belief prevailed that a practice could persist on Dutch soil in perpetuity after being condemned as barbaric everywhere else. The very thought of whites doing manual labor scandalized the colonists, and the prospect of free laborers, white and colored, competing as equals was enough to ensure their utter rejection of the plan. Under the pretext "that contact with a society corrupted by the system of slavery could adversely affect the morality of the new agriculturalists,"[94] they rejected any location that would have qualified because of its favorable natural setting, and instead chose the deserted plantation of Voorzorg, somewhere out in the jungle. The planned settlement was then constructed by an opponent of colonization, who saved 250 guilders on each dwelling, proceeded as slowly as possible, put the immigration process in the hands of a couple of pastors instead of agricultural experts, and hoped that everything would turn out for the best, God willing, when the colonists – who in any case were nothing more than poor proletarians from the mother country – finally got there.

Poor Baron van Raders – no sooner had he arrived in the colony, on October 9, 1845, than it fell to him to liquidate this failed enterprise! He had barely had time to earn the everlasting hatred of many colonists, by forbidding them to drive away with whips the slaves who came to hear the music at his inauguration, when he was told, at Voorzorg, the facts quoted below from the *History of Suriname*:

> On the morning of June 21, 1845, the ship *Susanne Maria* reached Voorzorg, but what a disappointment awaited the hopeful colonists there! Little progress had been made with the preliminary measures for their reception; the fifty thousand guilders spent on them might as well have been thrown away. A few huts with straw (palm leaf) roofs, some still only half built, in a straight line against the green horizon of impenetrable forest, made an unappealing sight for the colonists. When their ship had laid anchor, chilling scenes had been played out on board: women and children

wailing and shrieking, men pacing the deck in anger and desperation when they saw where they had been sent. Most of them refused to disembark; a few, who still had some money, offered it to the captain to take them back ... And if the houses were wretched, there was also a lack of furniture, a lack of everything. Not one square foot of land had been cultivated or made arable.

They could not hope to bake bread; the oven was broken and there was no kneading trough. The colonists were obliged to subsist primarily on spekkoeken.[95] ... There was not enough accommodation for all of them in Voorzorg, and those who remained there lived seven to ten to a house, while the others moved into the buildings of the former Groningen military base across the river.

The unhealthy accommodation, poor diet, and disappointment, which had come as such a shock to all of them, led to a wave of illness. This soon claimed several lives; the medical assistance of a ship's surgeon with a medicine chest was inadequate. The compelling words of Pastor Copijn persuaded the colonial administration to send help ... Physicians, apothecaries, and caretakers hurried to their aid; ferries loaded with medicine and nourishment were sent there; but all this was in vain, it was too late! ... In only a few months, more than half the newly arrived colonists had died, including the beloved and lamented Pastor Copijn. That was the state of affairs when Van Raders reached Groningen on October 15, 1845.[96]

An admirable way to begin, and what happened next was just as admirable. While Van Raders, in Paramaribo, was doing his best to help the colonists by putting livestock and hired-out slaves at their disposal, the leader of the colony, Pastor Arend van den Brandhof, was using part of this slave force to erect a beautiful villa for himself in the Italian style, where he spent his time taking care of paperwork, working at his desk, and shouting the occasional order from the veranda without ever taking the trouble to oversee the farmers' work with his own two eyes.

And, even so, the soil surprised the colonists with its fertility. But a few months after the first rains, when they had all harvested greens and root vegetables, they found they could not sell them for a good price in Paramaribo because their means of transportation were inadequate. This was the colony's undoing; some fifty thousand guilders had been thrown away.

A different variety of white settlement was tested by the firm of Kreglinger & Co. along the Maroni in 1852. This time the settlers were from Württemberg and went there to work as loggers. The outcome proved that this type of initiative was economically and financially feasible. After 37,000 guilders of capital had been invested, the revenue from sales of wood in the first year alone was 21,000 guilders. Nevertheless, the firm refused to invest any more, so, in the absence of financial support from the colonial administration, the project had to be terminated. This reluctance to continue, even after such a promising start, has a deeper explanation: the settlement's leader, August Kappler, was in continual conflict with his workers, who refused to be exploited like Negro slaves. These workers had the support of Bühler, "who had had a scientific education but was full of red socialist ideas." Bühler was summoned by the authorities in Paramaribo and ordered to leave the country, but before he could depart, he died of the yellow fever then rampant in the city. The fear that his ideas had not died with him was undoubtedly one factor behind the drastic liquidation of the whole settlement, which could have had such great significance to the evolution of working conditions in Suriname. For in those days, the colonial government saw the greatest threat not in the maroons but in European proletarians, who might have shown their black brothers that a worker is not necessarily a slave.

Fighting the Current

There are people whose work you can scrutinize from every angle without finding a single place where they have fallen short, people of great diligence, attentiveness, and devotion to duty, whose competence and insight is beyond question, but who nonetheless achieve nothing lasting, leaving behind only the abandoned remains of the projects they embarked on with such passion. They are the people who try with all their might to row against a current stronger than they, which dashes their boat against the rocks and swiftly wrecks it, to the mocking laughter of the crowd. Such a man, no doubt, was Baron van Raders. He arrived in a colony where the emancipation of the slaves was thought to be impossible because freed slaves would refuse to perform any manual labor, their past having poisoned the idea of manual labor for them by linking it unbreakably to slavery. And he, as governor, was not above taking up the digger's shovel himself to put an end to this pernicious idea. The construction, by free workers, of the canal to Kwatta, which began with the rerouting of Steenbakkersgracht, was the first act of great moral significance by a Dutch governor, in that it punctured the prejudice against outdoor labor once and for all. And, once again, we must report that the completion of the project – which would have opened the way to settlement by sixty white farm families – was prevented by the obstructionism of the colonial administration. Van Raders put five thousand guilders of his own into the project, to no avail. He strove to introduce maize cultivation in Suriname, to no avail. He endeavored to improve stock breeding by growing para grass, to no avail. He tried to introduce reforms in response to the West Indian bank affair, to no avail. At every turn he met with blind, stealthy opposition, and his opponents would sooner have witnessed the colony's utter downfall than allow a man like Van Raders the least success.

For Van Raders was the man who dared to adopt shorter working hours for slaves on the government sugar plantation Catharina Sophia, making production not fall but rise from three and a half hogsheads in a long-drawn-out day to five in ten hours. Van Raders gave them shoes, doing away with "the main signs of slavery."[97] Van Raders prohibited the transportation of slaves from one plantation to the other. Van Raders tried to persuade plantation administrators to treat their slaves less harshly.[98]

This type of idealist is dangerous; this type of maniac trespasses on the rights of the slaveholders; this type of dreamer must be crushed. So the dreamer, whose worst crime was that he was not merely a dreamer, but a capable man of action, was crushed. A trivial diplomatic incident was sufficient pretext for his involuntary dismissal in 1852.

He was a man of character.

Governors on Parade

On August 28, 1833, the slaves in the British colonies were fully emancipated.

France followed the British example in 1848. It was not until July 1, 1863, that the Netherlands was forced to follow suit in its colony of Suriname.

We will now take a close look at the governors to see with what degree of resolve and dedication they prepared for emancipation.

Baron van Raders was followed by Johann George Otto Stuart von Schmidt auf Altenstadt, a sickly man lacking force of will, a puppet of the reactionaries. He had one sole passion: cutting public expenditure. The historical record shows that "he left behind a decaying mess, which cost

three times the sum of his so-called economies to set right."
Under the pressure of public opinion in the Netherlands,
the regulations on slavery were improved in a few respects
during his term of office, but these changes were minor
and, what is more, the planters ignored them.

After Schmidt auf Altenstadt resigned, in 1855, the new
governor was Charles Pierre Schimpf. Just as this major
general's name was a mixture of French and German
sounds, his official acts were a mixture of good and evil,
with the evil becoming more clearly dominant over time,
until he was entirely under the influence of the reactionary
party.

Under Schimpf, many profitable positions went to friends
and acquaintances. Under Schimpf, foolish wastefulness
replaced his predecessor's idiotic austerity. Under Schimpf,
the slave regulations became empty words, and alongside
flogging, forced labor was introduced as another form of
punishment. This did not prevent Schimpf from claiming
in an official report to the government that "slavery exists
only in name in Suriname."

Under Schimpf, the forest patrols were sent out again,
runaway slaves were flogged, and the regulations on
slavery were flouted to such a degree that "the punishment
for abuse of power by the masters existed more in name
than in reality."[99]

But it was under Schimpf, most of all, that the tragedy
took place that would reveal what awaited Suriname after
the abolition of legal slavery.

In 1858, at the insistence of a number of planters, who
believed immigration was needed before slavery could be
abolished, five hundred Chinese coolies were rounded up
through the offices of the Dutch consul in Macao. But
when they arrived in Suriname in April, it appeared that no
one wanted to hire coolies when they could force slaves to

toil for nothing. At this, the contract entered into with the Chinese workers was modified by the governor's authority in favor of the employers.

The Chinese were treated as slaves in every respect. When they protested, they were caned by the police without any form of trial – a violation of the regulations in force – and this illegal act was repeated again and again.

The Dutch parliament questioned the minister of colonies, Jan Jacob Rochussen, but it did not help. The contract entered into with the Dutch consul was not upheld. The treatment of the Chinese was unjust. They were not slaves by law, but the gap between the legal and the real was large enough to hold the entire difference between law and power, between human dignity and the thirst for profit.

Then, in 1859, Governor Reinhart Frans van Lansberge took charge of the colony. He had the dubious distinction of quelling another full-scale slave revolt with force of arms rather late in the nineteenth century, in 1861. That year in the district of Coronie, many slaves left their masters and attempted to reach Demerara, where they hoped to gain their freedom under the British regime. The colonial government in Suriname sent a so-called white commission with troops to subdue the revolt, and the prisoners were treated in the most barbaric way.

Slaves also revolted on the timber estate of Berg en Dal along the upper reaches of the Suriname river. There too, the so-called white commission and its troops were sent to put down the revolt.

On that occasion, the church – which still owns large tracts of land in Suriname – demonstrated that the colonial regime had nothing to fear from it. It thus corrected the grave mistake made in 1848 by Otto Tank, the leading Moravian missionary in Suriname, when he had the audacity to expose the horrors of slavery in a circular addressed to slaveholders and administrators in the Netherlands.[100] To avoid the accusation that we are casting the church in too nefarious a role here, let us turn for a few moments to an enthusiastic admirer of missionary work, who wrote:

> Tank never returned to Suriname again, and since that time the Moravians have even more strictly adhered to the established rule of holding their tongues about such matters. In order not to lose everything, they had to make many concessions to the slaveholders (including the profanation of the sacrament of marriage, in that slaves were prohibited by law from marrying!). In return for the opportunity to give those slaves a few drops from the full cup of the Gospels, they agreed to remain silent, a silence sometimes difficult to maintain. So we shall not denounce those dear brothers, even though we firmly believe it was often their duty to speak.[101]

As long as slavery was condoned by law in the colony, missionary work was tolerated among the Indian tribes, which were relatively unimportant. The conversion of the Negroes, in contrast, was opposed with the greatest vigor, because white pride could not tolerate the thought of slaves having the same religion as their masters. From 1668 to 1854, when the thirty-six Dutch Reformed (Nederlands Hervormd) preachers in Paramaribo used the word "brothers," they always meant people of their own skin color. That was truly how they saw the cultural mission of the Netherlands in the colony. It was not until the end of slavery came into sight that the Christianization of the blacks by the whole spectrum of Dutch denominations came to be seen as a way of sowing dissension among them. It was not until slavery was abolished that the Bible was taken up to foster the same obedience on spiritual grounds. And such missionary work was only permitted because it was firmly believed that every missionary, to a man, sincerely believed in the Christian principle of obedience to the God-appointed authorities. Yet Christian principles were so abjectly betrayed in what men of God dared to write about the revolt on Rac à Rac Plantation: that plantation slaves had been known to rise up before in response to perceived injustice, but that the act of leaving the director's home without any reason for dissatisfaction was more than outrageous.

The Abolition of Slavery

On July 1, 1863, a twenty-one-gun salute sounded to mark the legal abolition of slavery in Suriname. The cannons were probably fired by the new troops sent to the colony in large numbers to prepare for the festivities. In any case, they were a stark echo of the shots fired such a short time before, in the autumn of 1862, by Captain Steenberghe's soldiers.

This battle and the events leading up to it deserve the full attention of anyone who still has too many illusions about the motives of the Netherlands in "freeing" the slaves. Once it had become clear that Suriname could not maintain the anachronism of slavery while situated between two emancipated colonies to which the slaves trickled away as if through the bottom of a leaky barrel, efforts were naturally made to ensure that the emancipation process would have the most beneficial possible outcome. State commissions of 1853 and 1861 were charged with squaring the circle – in other words, with investigating how slavery could be abolished without the slaveholders suffering any losses.

Considering that more than one hundred thousand (100,000) Surinamese people had done hard labor for the Netherlands as slaves for three and a half centuries and been paid nothing for it, who could call it unjust if the Surinamese people made a claim against the mother country that owed its colony's prosperity to this inhumane system? It is understandable that the commission, which of course did not include any son of our race, looked solely at the interest of the wealthy slaveholders and concluded that they should be compensated for each freed slave in the amount of three hundred (300) guilders. The next step was to take inventory as soon as possible. The more slaves, the more silver. Commissions were formed to register the slaves, determine their age (approximately), and throw in a complimentary Dutch name. This was how Jansen, Krijnsen, De Kom, and other such euphonious names took the place of Jaw, Kodjo, Abenibo, and the like, which we inherited from our fathers.

But when the time came, greed awakened in the heart of many plantation owners. Why, they would receive three hundred guilders for each slave, and then to think that there were hundreds of maroons roaming the forests who had once been their lawful property and for whom they would not receive a cent ... What an injustice! And the colonial administration, which must have had a surplus of funds, tried to lend the plantation owners a helping hand by promising all maroons amnesty in a publication of October 20, 1862. When that did not help, this message followed: "All slaves who escaped in earlier or later years or in recent times are guaranteed that they will not be punished for their escape. Those born in the camps of the fugitives may likewise return without fear to their masters or to the plantations known to them as those of their mothers or grandmothers."[102] It sounded very fine indeed. But the maroons, probably sensing what sort of freedom was in store for them, declined to walk into the trap of their own accord. And sure enough, when sweet whistling was not enough to lure the birdies in, when Van Lansberge's rousing promises of freedom did not draw enough volunteers, the next step, in 1862, was an expedition into the forest to capture the runaway slaves. The colonial administration sent out a certain Captain Steenberghe to attempt to make the maroons return. This led to pitched combat, and the whites were forced into immediate retreat.

When the governor heard the news, he sent reinforcements: white colonial troops to help Steenberghe's soldiers destroy the camp. Steenberghe had barely reached the forest when the rebels opened heavy fire, killing a number of whites. The soldiers returned fire and even turned the navy's swivel guns on the rebels, who were nonetheless able to escape to safety with their wounded. Steenberghe had to abandon his mission. Thanks to him, the last chapter of legal slavery, like the others, was written in blood.

Immediately following emancipation, the colonial administration, through the offices of the Moravian brother Johannes Drexler, made peace with the maroons.

Freedom?

"What, after all," Linguet pondered:

> did society gain in place of slavery? What is known as free servitude. But the gift of emancipation, in this fashion, is nothing more than the wreath used to adorn the victim, an utter mockery. Even slavery is better and gentler than that. Since the essence of society is that the rich do not work, servitude is merely a gentle name for a still harsher reality than slavery was. At least a slave was fed, even when he did not work, just as all our horses had hay in the rack in those days. But what becomes of the free day laborer, who is generally paid badly for his work, what becomes of him if he has no work? He is free – but that very freedom is his misfortune! He belongs to no one, but no one cares about him. When he is needed, he is hired for the lowest possible wage. This promised pittance is barely enough to pay for

his food on the day he works. Supervisors are appointed to force him to complete his work punctually; they make him hurry, they goad him on, in fear that he will find some way to conceal half his strength so that he can remain at work longer. His employer, in his grasping desire to economize, watches with a restless expression as he works, heaps reproaches on him whenever he seems to allow himself the slightest pause, and, if he ever stops to rest for a moment, accuses him of stealing. When the work is done he is sent away as abruptly as he was summoned, with the chilliest sort of indifference, and no one stops to wonder whether the twenty or thirty small coins he earned with his bitter day's work will allow him to provide for himself, should he happen to find no work the next day.[103]

Even now, there is a great deal of truth in Linguet's words, even if every year the day of emancipation, July 1, is still celebrated in Suriname with a great display of joy.

Prove to us, if you can, that the Surinamese are free in the true meaning of the word, that they are no longer forced to sell their capacity for labor, albeit in a different manner than in the era of slavery.

We say to you that the physical instruments of torture have been largely replaced with mental torments, poverty, and want. It is as if we were pulled out of the fire only to be hurled into the waves of the Atlantic, unable to swim. For it is foolish to suppose that people who had been kept muzzled for centuries, and then were suddenly left with no means of support and without even a patch of land, were truly prepared to live in freedom. The many millions that slaves were forced to earn with their blood and sweat were used for the benefit of the white slaveholders, while the downtrodden, the oppressed, were left to their fate.

What would Suriname have been without the labor of the slaves? And yet nothing was done for these Surinamese people at the time of their supposed emancipation; no concessions were made to the needs of the poor freedmen;

on the contrary, the whole emancipation of the slaves was designed to leave the freedmen with no other choice than to return voluntarily to the slavery that had just been abolished by law.

While the colonists received three hundred guilders per slave, the freed slaves themselves had not one red cent to call their own. They were free, but without the means to provide for themselves for a single day. They were given no land, as the European colonists had been. They were given no agricultural training that would later have enabled them to cultivate their smallholdings. They were given no credit with which they might have become tenant farmers and purchased the tools necessary for working the land.

The only thing they were given was the warning that all plantation slaves from the ages of fifteen to sixty were required to enter into coolie contracts for the performance of plantation labor. Those who lived in the city (city slaves) were required to enter into domestic labor contracts. Their wages were, of course, determined for them and without them. That was how "freedom" looked under so-called "state supervision."[104]

The Great Sellout

You, Dutch readers, learned in your school days that the emancipation of the slaves led to the downfall of the previously wealthy colony of Suriname. There is no better way to debunk this myth than by once again quoting that great expert on the colony, J. Wolbers. Describing the situation there a few years before the abolition of slavery, he writes:

> Certain individuals did enjoy material advantages under the system of slavery, but they were few in number, and a thorough review of the historical sources, the results of

which have been reported here, has left me completely certain that Suriname never truly flourished or knew any solid prosperity; and now, while slavery continues in a possession of the Netherlands, disgracing the name of the Netherlands, trade and agriculture in the colony are languishing. While sugar production has expanded in recent years and yields considerable revenue, other crops have been more or less abandoned, and the expansion of the sugar industry has come at the cost of the health and the lives of the slave workforce. The number of slaves, Suriname's productive force, has steadily – except in a few good years – declined. Over the many years that uncertainty and indecision about this situation have prevailed, the spirit of enterprise has been extinguished. Although some are unconcerned and go on wringing the slaves dry for the sake of continued material profits, reasoning "Après nous, le déluge," or saying with carefree frivolity, like the fool in Scripture, "Let us eat and drink, for tomorrow we die," the better people, the core of the free population, join us in yearning for the abolition of slavery, since slavery stands in the way of all development, and if that ruinous system goes on any longer, Suriname must fall.[105]

Likewise, the supposed laziness of the freed slaves is sufficiently refuted by one R.E. in the Surinamese weekly of September 23, 1860:

It is a certainty that the poverty of freedmen is not always the result of laziness. In 1860, a few freedmen even offered to perform the spadework, the most demanding plantation work, but they found no employers who would accept their offer, despite the fact that slaveholders so often complain of a shortage of workers. Whereas the freedmen had overcome the prejudice against plantation work, the planter could not tolerate free people working alongside his slaves. So we cannot hope for any improvement in this respect until slavery has been abolished.

This hope proved to be in vain. Why? Because all the humanists who reasoned this way were overlooking the mentality of the ruling class, which remained constant regardless of any changes in the law, a mentality of such licentiousness and dissolution that, in 1858, 83 legitimate and 255 illegitimate children were born to them, and Wolbers was pained to describe "men who have relations with seven or eight slave women at a time, who send one packing today and pick a new one tomorrow, while the slave women have no choice but to give in to the lusts of their masters." This mentality itself was another product of slavery, as he was right to note: "That abominable system demoralizes not only the slaves, but also the free."[106] People with such a mentality were not suited or equipped to take the colony's economic life in a new direction in the new era. The money that they received for their slaves merely gave them the perfect opportunity to withdraw from all everyday cares and woes, leave their plantations behind, and flaunt their newly acquired capital in the mother country.

Most plantation owners and managers feared that after emancipation their large profits and dividends would evaporate. They began to divest themselves of their holdings, selling them off to any vulture who made a reasonable offer. On the sugar plantations, for example, the orders came down to pull up or crush all the sugarcane, ripe or unripe. On the coffee plantations, the bushes were removed from the soil roots and all. The capital fled abroad, so that time after time even the meager wages could not be paid. One plantation after another was transformed into a wilderness and, where work was still done, it was done under such extreme conditions that when the period of state supervision ended, the workers deserted en masse. The colony's downfall is to be blamed not on the slaves' laziness but on their masters' greed!

The Era of "Freedom"

How We Live

> Those who are frightened can never reach the innermost part of my country.
>
> Albert Helman

Go for a walk, dear Dutch readers – on a day without rain, if you can – through the streets of Paramaribo, unpaved but broad and planted with tamarind, orange, and palm trees. Admire the stately stone town houses built along the streets by the property owners in various centuries, and then go, if you can muster the courage, through the Negro gate onto the grounds. On either side of a muddy path lie the old, neglected one-room hovels of the former slaves, now home to the free proletarians of Suriname.

> No drains, no electric light, no running water in these houses.
>
> Somewhere at the far end of the property is a broken-down privy.
>
> Everything you see bespeaks poverty and deprivation. Very little has changed here since slavery was abolished.[1]

148

Then pick up the July 21, 1931, issue of *De Banier* and read a brief announcement (submitted on July 18) by the subcommittee for child nutrition:[2] "On Monday, the 20th of this month, the distribution of food to undernourished schoolchildren will begin. The truck transporting the food will begin its rounds at 12:30 p.m. We have learned that approximately 1,800 children at twenty-four schools have been registered, but for the time being food can be supplied only to 900."

The son of Suriname, the dark-skinned man, wants to live, to live at any price, to live, as much as anyone else does, even if he must perform the heaviest labor, brave the greatest hardships, sign the most exploitative contract, and work under conditions never yet seen in any agreement ever made between people living in true freedom.

On one side stands the Surinamese proletarian, with no property whatsoever to his name, a worker with nothing to sell but his labor.

On the other side stands the Balata Compagnie, "the mainstay of the colony," the darling of the administration until the economic crisis of 1931, since when this final source of wealth under the capitalist production system is in danger of drying up like all the others.

The Balata Compagnie presents the Negro with its livret. Although the terms of this voluminous legal code, compiled by the company directors in their absolute power, have never been endorsed by any popular assembly or ratified by any parliament, compliance is enforced by every organ of the state, by the police, and by the army.

And the Negro signs.

"In complete freedom" he places his signature, then his thumbprint, on the contract, and from that moment on the difference between the slave of bygone days and the voluntary contracting party of the present is really not so great.

Until the last day of his contract, the Negro is required to carry out every task assigned to him precisely as instructed. The company has the right "to terminate this contract at any time, even in the absence of 'compelling reasons' as specified by law, on the condition that the worker receives compensation in the amount of ten guilders" (art. 2).

The Negro lives in a camp that is like a barracks, does not have the right to let friends, acquaintances, or even his wife into his place of residence, is not permitted to leave his place of work for any reason without the written permission of his supervisor, and is required to remain in the areas designated by the responsible supervisor at all times.

The Negro "is required not only to gather balata in compliance with any system whatsoever, but also to carry out any other work assigned to him by the Compagnie or in its name ... He will receive no payment for the afore-mentioned tasks if they are in the direct interest of his own person or work, as, for instance, if he is building his own camp, making his dry grounds and dabrees, or cutting the lines he needs for his own balata collecting" (art. 3).[3]

Also unpaid is the transportation of the balata he has collected. He provides all the transportation and assistance for free when one of his workmates is struck down by illness or a work-related accident. In any dispute, the company directs him to the colonial court, which the May 26, 1931, issue of *De Banier* described in the following terms:

> What jurisdiction did the court have in this matter? Can this be called the unbiased administration of justice? If the population has no confidence in the justice administered in the Name of the Queen (!), it will have less still in the decisions of the executive authorities.
>
> Unlucky country, to be unable to have unconditional confidence in the integrity of the people who govern it!

The Negro is a propertyless proletarian, required to buy his food, equipment, and tools in the Compagnie store at prices set unilaterally by the Compagnie.

The Compagnie, in contrast, "retains the full authority to refuse the worker additional food and equipment that are not strictly necessary in the opinion of the Compagnie and has no obligation to keep any items in stock aside from those required by law" (art. 13).

The Negro has no right to food from the time he signs the contract to the day he leaves for his workplace. The costs of food are his to pay, even in the case of illness. But the length of the working day, at least eight hours, is determined by the supervisor, who has the sole power to decide if a sufficient quantity of work has been performed. Under these conditions the Negro works, in the unhealthiest wildlands, for a wage of f 1.25 (one guilder and twenty-five cents) a day.

Under these elastic yet binding constraints he labors, under threat of a f 2.50 fine any time he commits any one of the following violations:

> ... disorderly conduct; failure to comply promptly with orders issued to him by the employer, inspector, or supervisor; vulgarity; reckless endangerment of himself or others; loss or wastage of drinking or washing water; and any other acts that contravene or breach the terms of this contract and are not punishable under the statutory provisions in force in the colony. (art. 26)

Under these conditions he works until compelled by the expiration of his contract or by illness to go to the city by whatever mode of transport is chosen for him, whether on foot, by rail, or by boat!

We will not speak here of the interpretation of these articles, of arbitrariness and fraud in the weighing and inspection of the balata collected, all of which we experienced time and again in the employ of this company. We merely present the terms of the contract that Suriname's supposedly autonomous bleeders – who are first-class professionals – not only sign but also seal with their thumbprint (as if they were criminals!).

We ask the Dutch trade union leaders: what would you say to such provisions as a model for collective agreements for whites?

We ask the Dutch workers: slavery has been abolished in Suriname, but can you call those who are forced to work under such a contract truly free? And to think that this contract is a model of good practice compared to many used by bauxite and other companies, or on plantations.

The Essence of Autonomy

We have jumped ahead in history for a moment in order to produce convincing evidence of how relative a thing human freedom is, even now, seventy years later, for proletarians in Suriname. Now we will take up the thread of our chronological narrative once more and, at the risk of boring the reader with too long a series of names and facts, go on analyzing Dutch colonization from year to year and revealing the characteristics of this regime.

Slavery had been abolished. Colonial society was in need of a new order. It was time to lay the foundations for a different future. What epithet was earned by the third Dutch governor to take this Atlantean task upon his shoulders? He was known as the "lean" Baron van Heerdt, with his wizened budgets, about which his proudest boast was "that his projections of expenditure were not permitted to exceed what was necessary to keep the services in operation." An ideal governor, to those whose fondest wish was to see public spending cut back to a bare minimum. But his impact is undeniable when we read that under his administration, in healthy Suriname, severe epidemics of dysentery, whooping cough, and malaria felled the undernourished inhabitants; out of a population of 23,000, more than three hundred died in sixty days, and it was not unusual for more than fifteen people to be buried in a single day. Yet why such indignation about a few governors? Why not commemorate the fact that as early as 1866, the enlightened Dutch nation granted Suriname that which others now yearn for in vain: "autonomy, the sacred right of the people to self-determination!"?

Let us not be too quick to applaud, let us not be dazzled by a name, as if a Labor Council, for instance, were the same thing as a workers' council.[4] Let us not settle for the mere word but first inquire how Surinamese autonomy actually looks.

The colonial apparatus of Suriname works as follows: the colony forms an unbreakable whole with the unitary Dutch kingdom.[5] The governor is appointed by the king and is also the supreme commander of the armed forces. When the governor introduces new laws, he is assisted by:

1. A Governing Council (of Dutchmen), of which the governor is the chairman, the chief public prosecutor is the deputy chair, the financial administrator is a member, and the secretary of the colonial administration is the secretary. As we can see, all these members are officials appointed by the king, and the two other members of this body are also royal appointees.

2. The Colonial States, which are said to represent the Surinamese people. Four of this body's members are chosen by enfranchised citizens, which is to say those who pay taxes over an annual income of at least 1,400 guilders. In practical terms, this means that the large majority of the population is excluded from having any influence on the administration of the colony.

Yet this entire legislative branch of government is a sham, in that these bodies are denied the most important right: that of budgetary oversight. For it always has been and is still the case that whenever an appropriation is made from the national coffers, the governor cannot present the Colonial States with anything more than a "provisional budget," on which the Dutch legislature – which is to say Pastor Kersten, Mr. Braat, and other such Suriname specialists – has the final say.[6] So in reality, little is left of Suriname's "autonomy." The truth is that every piece of legislation must be approved in the Netherlands, and the Netherlands appoints the people who make the real decisions about the colony. As the May 25, 1931, issue of the colonial *Nieuws- en Advertentieblad Suriname* (Suriname News and Advertising Journal) accurately observed:

White and Brown. The ancient Greeks knew only of Greeks and barbarians; the Dutch in Suriname's civil service today know only of white people and brown people. The whites and a privileged other few live in luxury, and three large ethnic groups – indigenous people, British Indians, and the Javanese – are also permitted to lead comfortable lives, by Asian standards. Day by day the gap grows wider between white and brown. Salary is not linked to job description; suitability and competence are not the main requirements; instead, skin color is the primary qualification. The established system of rewarding employees who hold a European degree serves solely to benefit the Dutch. There are a few offices where the Surinamese are allowed to profit along with the whites, but if there are no Dutch employees who can reap the benefits of holding a European degree, then Surinamese employees need not try. They will be informed in the clearest possible terms that their department functions perfectly well without such a degree, and those brown and black people with European degrees will not be granted any extra salary. The department can get by with employees who don't have those European degrees. Every department of the Surinamese civil service can get by with employees educated here. Every position held by a Dutch employee with a European diploma can be filled, temporarily or permanently, by a Surinamese employee – in other words, by someone educated here – to the benefit of the department.

But this is not the worst of it. The June 9, 1931, issue of the newspaper *De Banier* states:

> Since the arrival of the current Governor, it must be observed that, just as the Fatherland Club formed by the Dutch uses its influence against the colored people there, many white people in Suriname use their influence against the colored people here.[7] Recruiters give preference to people from Indonesia for service in this colony, whether as public officials or in private companies.[8] Colored people, however competent and qualified they may be, usually lose out to the Surinamese European Group.

We therefore ask for the right to revisit the deeds, over the course of history, that have given these missionaries of European culture their moral superiority. And we soon run into a very typical specimen: Governor Jonkheer Maurits Adriaan de Savornin Lohman, who succeeded Hendrik Jan Smidt on January 30, 1889.[9] So to see the nineteenth century out in style, we will devote somewhat lengthier consideration to this period.

Fin de siècle

No sooner had authority changed hands than it became clear what heights of prosperity the former slaves had reached since their emancipation. After the ten-year transition period of state supervision had ended, those who no longer could or had to tolerate slave life on the plantations had become farmers with smallholdings for which they paid high tenancy fees to the owners or the government. (Even today, the tenancy fee paid to the colonial administration for uncultivated land is ten guilders per hectare *per month*.) But they also had to pay high taxes, which left them not much better off than the plantation proletarians. When it proved completely impossible for them to pay these taxes, De Savornin Lohman gave the small farmers along Para Creek six additional months to pay the personal taxes due by the first of April under the ordinance of February 9, 1886. But six months later the small farmers were as poor as ever, and since there is nothing new under the sun, they decided, even without Gandhi, to refuse to pay the tax. This led to their prosecution, and the court in its ingenuity ordered six hundred penniless Para residents to pay not only their taxes but also a large fine. When they did not pay either, the governor sent out District Commissioner Lionarons with a force of colonial troops under the command of Lieutenant Schut, with orders to throw the disobedient extremists in prison. But, when it became apparent that in the meantime the Para residents had taken up weapons and were prepared to put up the greatest possible resistance, the colonial force made the sensible choice, going into retreat without a single feat of arms.

What happened next was an outstanding example of autonomy in practice. The Colonial States had become curious about this conflict and requested information about the course of events, information which the governor refused outright to provide. The peculiar result was that all ordinances presented to the States by the governor were either rejected or not even debated, while De Savornin Lohman, for his part, refused to respond to any of the States' questions. To make matters worse, the governor summoned four members of the States to his palace: Johan Cateau van Rosevelt, head of the immigration service; Barnet Lyon, a public prosecutor; Dr. Salomons, a medical inspector; and Isaac da Costa, a circuit court judge. There he scolded them, in the presence of the colonial secretary Fockens, for having the nerve to ask His Excellency for information about Para Creek. At this point, the members of the States recalled that Suriname also had a populace, and each party, through its associated daily newspaper, tried to win over public opinion. On one side was *De Volksbode*, said to be subsidized by the governor and the vicar apostolic of Suriname, Monsignor Wilhelmus Wulfingh; on the other side, *De West-Indiër* fought like a fury. The remarkable thing was what came to light as a result of this infighting: revelations that were especially damaging to the religious denominations. Anitri lerimans and their Church (the Stichting Moravische Broeders in Zeist) sided with the governor and were accused of "diligently catching souls so that they could even more diligently rake in grant money." But the Moravian brothers returned the ball, leveling their own accusations at the Lutheran Church, which they claimed was turning one hundred heathens into Christians daily, merely in order to put that old proverb into practice: "The early bird catches the worm." Meanwhile, the chief public prosecutor Jan Kalff complained to the Dutch government, upon which the governor demanded, unsuccessfully, that Kalff be recalled to the Netherlands.

This was the situation as May 12 approached, the day when the 25th anniversary of the colonial charter would be celebrated. Tempers rose higher and higher. Weeks in advance, *De Volksbode* urged the populace not to take part in the festivities.

And the people, who took not the slightest interest in this whole struggle over jobs, poured into Paramaribo by the thousands and, on the day of the festivities, began to destroy all the decorations and other preparations in a surge of pent-up bitterness. Then the people were treated to the sight of the crowd driving away the police in the approving presence of the Dutch governor, De Savornin Lohman, who even ordered some of the military posts set up here and there to withdraw. If not for the downpour that hit Paramaribo on the evening of May 12, De Savornin Lohman's response would undoubtedly have transformed the city into a scene of boundless chaos and probably even into a bloodbath.

The hangover came soon enough. The very next day, the governor granted permission to go ahead with the celebration, and the day after that, the police used armed force against the massed people; their commander, Deputy Inspector Van Lierip, personally shot a Surinamese person dead for not stepping aside fast enough. A message sent to His Majesty by the Colonial States and the chief public prosecutor resulted in orders to the governor to work together with the police, the army, and the navy to re-establish law and order. He did so with fervor. And the Surinamese had learned the lesson that if you must fight, the only thing worth fighting for is your own self-interest.

Indentured Labor

"Free" labor = crumbs thrown to the masses.

Multatuli

The British Indians

The regulation of immigration is closely connected to economic conditions.

Insofar as such regulation is aimed at supplying workers for the plantations, supply will adjust itself to demand.

With respect to the further-reaching objective of settlement through immigration, there is no reason to put a stop to this; there are simply grounds for going forward at a slow pace. With this in mind, only one hundred and twenty families were brought to the colony in 1931. In this context, one bright side of the current coffee crisis should be pointed out: it contributes greatly to the transition to free labor. The insight that coffee cultivation, because it involves seasonal labor, is more economical with free workers than with indentured, is rapidly gaining ground, and the circumstances of our times are already making this reduction in cost price a reality. There is also the certainty that free workers – who are actually higher in quality than the indentured workers – can be brought directly from Java. That makes it possible to expand the free labor market, not only now but also in the future.

In the course of this year, thanks to cooperation between the Administration and the planters, another substantial shift toward free labor can be expected. It is my firm conviction that this will place coffee culture on a healthier footing and lead to a lasting reduction in cost price, thanks in no small part to the successful efforts of Noordhoek Hegt, the current Agent-General, to promote free immigration.

These were the words of Suriname's governor in a speech delivered at the opening of the Colonial States on Tuesday, May 12, 1931. "Another substantial shift toward free labor can be expected." What do you call the other kind, now that slavery has been abolished – or hasn't it? That kind is called indentured labor and is done largely by coolies imported from China, India, or Indonesia.

We have written earlier in this book about the Chinese tragedy. It did not tempt the experimenters to repeat the experiment quickly. Instead, they decided to try their luck with British Indians, who were expected to be less intelligent and less rebellious than the Chinese. To that end, the Netherlands concluded a treaty with the United Kingdom on September 8, 1870, during the tenure of Governor Van

Idsinga, regarding the immigration of coolies from British India to Suriname, and on June 5, 1873, the first ship of coolies reached Paramaribo. Many Dutch hearts began to beat a little faster now that the old slave trade appeared to be coming back to life in this new form. The slave drivers' methods also seemed to be coming back to life; in a message received on October 8, 1876, the immigration agent in Calcutta announced that Britain had suspended the emigration of coolies.

Great consternation.

Investigation by a government commission.

And Agent-General Cateau van Rosevelt reported that the treatment of coolies in Suriname left nothing to be desired.

Britain was satisfied.

In February, emigration to Suriname was resumed.

"Their treatment leaves nothing to be desired." Well, then, let us first look at what sort of people these imported Hindus were. Helman writes about them in his book *Zuid Zuid-West* ("South South-West"):

> Don't be deceived by the boisterousness of the Hindus, who are almost all "coolies," because they are in essence silent and introverted. They seek a synthesis between outer and inner harmony. They are frugal and austere to such a degree that they seem the most impoverished of all people. The men walk around half naked with broad cloths on their skinny thighs. But on their festival days, they wear colorful overgarments of orange or pink silk, and their straight hair shines with oil.
>
> The women, in contrast, dress in very good taste, even on weekdays, and are very reserved beneath their veils, which glide around the passers-by in the streets like festive flags.
>
> In the outer districts, they stand out in front of their huts early every morning and wash themselves with great

care from scrubbed copper vessels. They rarely have many household effects other than these, and a divan of braided rope. They do not sleep on the ground, as the Negroes do. The silence of the fields they cultivate, the sunlight that skips across the low bushes and brings each leaf to maturity, fills them with the most wondrous thoughts. So they usually sing while working, or else hum couplets from the Vedas.

Their nakedness and poverty do not prevent them from knowing a great deal.

Could any people be more peaceable?

"Their treatment leaves nothing to be desired." But the proof of the pudding is in the eating and, as early as September 1884, the indentured coolies from India mounted their first large-scale revolt. The troops were swiftly mustered, the "extremists" attacked, and seven "rascals struck down." By this bloody, violent method, Governor Van Heerdt tot Eversberg soon suppressed the revolt. But where the flames had been extinguished, the embers smoldered still, and not long afterwards, in August 1891, the Hindustanis rose up in protest again. The police response was forceful; a few coolies were taken prisoner, and it seemed the resistance had been nipped in the bud, when all of a sudden coolies on several other plantations declared their solidarity with the rebels. This time, there were violent clashes with the armed forces, and by the time order was restored, two more coolies had been killed and many others wounded.

The wealthy planters, outraged, submitted a petition to the governor: "To put an end to this untenable situation, we call on the administration to help us combat the ruffianism of the British Indian immigrants."

At the same time, the plantation administrators and owners in Holland sent a similar request to the minister of colonies, demanding "that severe measures be taken against the ongoing resistance movement among the British Indian coolies." These petitions did not, of course, mention their grievances – which until then had generally fallen on deaf ears in the colonial administration – of maltreatment, backbreaking work, and obscenely low wages. But those grievances were expressed all the more clearly by the protests of the coolies themselves, who in their rancor now went from plantation to plantation, uprooting more than a thousand coffee plants. This culminated in a final battle between the coolies and the colonizers, in which the latter succeeded, thanks to superior weaponry, in crushing the resistance once and for all. The British Indians had learned in the most painful manner that their little group, in isolation from the rest of the people of Suriname, could not win the fight for better living conditions.

They adjusted to the circumstances as best they could, and Helman now writes:

> Hard labor in a tropical climate sometimes earns them enough to return to their tall old temples in Benares. But they usually die here, in the basement of a stinking hospital or the barracks of a remote plantation. The young people see a dull despair coming over them. No books of wisdom can save them any longer, and the beautiful poetry of their people only makes them more homesick. They cease to value each other's lives and murder over trivialities. They humor the admonishing pandit but do not love him.

The Indonesians[10]

Famine and want drove the exploited Indonesian coolies to leave the desa, follow the call of the recruiter, and seek a better life in Suriname. Like the British Indians, they saw their expectations disappointed. In August and November 1890, the first ninety-four Indonesians were imported. These poor wretches had been persuaded by the wealthy Dutch trading company, the Nederlandse Handel-Maatschappij, to toil for five years as indentured coolies on Mariënburg Plantation. They were found to be obedient laborers, and in June 1894, the first large group of Indonesian emigrants reached Paramaribo.

Of the 612 coolies packed like sardines into the ship's hold, thirty-two died on the voyage as a result of malnourishment, a lack of fresh air, and filthy berths. Sixteen more died before they could disembark, while the ship was anchored in Paramaribo's roadstead, and two hundred others were gravely ill and had to be admitted to the Military Hospital. Although these days the transports no longer claim so many lives, the conditions under which coolies are shipped to Suriname are still such that anyone who has experienced them looks back on them with the utmost rancor.

Once these Indonesians arrive on the plantations, they must do hard labor there in the burning sun without any hope of ever saving as much as ten guilders toward a return trip to their fatherland.

Do not misunderstand us. We Surinamese are not in any way opposed to truly free immigration of workers and poor farmers to a prosperous Suriname. Our country is large and rich enough, if governed well, to make many people prosperous. We are willing to grant the same rights to the Indonesians as to all workers. But we oppose the practice of exploiting the Indonesians' poverty and misery to persuade them, under false pretenses, to sign contracts that keep wages low and working conditions poor in Suriname and perpetuate the old slave mentality.

We also oppose the remarkable difference in treatment if ever a group of immigrants happens to be white instead of colored. In October 1892, around the time when these Indonesians crossed the oceans, Governor Titus van Asch van Wijk appointed a commission to investigate whether the settlement of Suriname by Europeans (particularly the Dutch) was desirable, what conditions would have to be met, and what forms of support would be necessary. How considerate of them to make such careful preparations!

Pamphlets like H. Pyttersen's were filled with useful tips for white emigrants. In February 1897, a number of Germans settled in Suriname to cultivate small farms. The government gave them everything they required, permitted them to seek out the best locations, and helped them to do so. We must point this out because those born in Suriname have never, ever, been treated with such generosity.

Above all, however, we protest the destitution into which the Indonesians are plunged as soon as their coolie contracts have expired. In an economic depression like the one we are going through now, this has especially evil consequences. The large agricultural companies set them loose, throng after throng, when they are barred even from applying for unemployment benefits, on the pretext that the so-called immigration department and the commissioners are responsible for their protection. But what form does this "protection" actually take? Its only apparent purpose is to ensure that, after all the effort devoted to pumping workers into the colony, it will not run dry again.[11] The Indonesian, lured there with the prospect of returning to his fatherland wealthy, must therefore have his hopes dashed. Reasons must be found to make his right to return to the Indies a mere illusion, so that there will be no need to pay him some sort of fee to waive that right.

For this purpose, the country's employers have worked in close partnership, especially since the measures taken by Alexander Cornelis Noordhoek Hegt, in the framework of their joint Surinamese immigration agency.

When a coolie is ill or exhausted, the district commissioner, who is usually also the deputy public prosecutor, may take him before the magistrate for "refusal to work." If he pays a brief visit to the neighboring plantation to talk to one of his countrymen about old times and former happiness, he runs the risk of being convicted of "desertion." If by unfortunate accident he damages a coffee plant or berry, it is deemed dereliction of another man's property. And he is punished for all these crimes with some period, long or short, of forced labor, known in our country by the proud title of "Public Works," at the same time forfeiting his right to repatriation. Oh, many a Saijah will never see his Adinda again![12]

The short-lived dream of happiness gave way to a long, long nightmare of misery.

And the current situation of the Javanese coolies certainly is a miserable one, which forces many of them onto the path of crime. The thefts and robberies that some of them commit are a true plague on the colony, while others who are less bold live on the proceeds of renting out the bodies of their wives and daughters.

Yet the colonial regime did not limit itself to so-called free contracts, but also used forced labor in its purest form to build roads and canals in Suriname, although we must acknowledge that this punishment was reserved for colored criminals.

"There are occasional complaints," *De Banier* wrote on July 7, 1931, "of inadequate policing in the capital, which has led to a rise in theft and burglary. But villains and burglars can, for the mere cost of keeping them imprisoned, be put to work constructing our roads." Perhaps they would not have become villains and criminals if, in the days when they were free laborers, they had been put to work on the same roads for decent pay.

The Creoles[13]

But indentured labor is not the exclusive privilege of new imports; the Suriname-born can also experience it by signing up to work for one of the Balata Compagnie subsidiaries or another large enterprise. We refer back to the livret discussed above and have a few more facts to report about their working methods and conditions.

The atmosphere around the departure pier is unusually hectic. Donkeys yoked to two-wheeled carts pull their loads slowly onward, unfazed by the urgings of the drivers. Men carry heavy trunks strapped to their backs. Beautiful women in colorful outfits with stiffly starched batik headscarves balance gleaming copper tubs of delicacies on their heads. They bought them for their fathers with their last stivers. The workers take their places among the cargo in the rowboats that will carry them on their several-day journey. Mother has already been kissed goodbye. "Tan bun," and they're off.

The next stage, some days later, is prospecting. This field investigation takes approximately four months to complete. An experienced laborer, who of course has a family to provide for in the city, is paid one guilder fifty a day plus expenses. The work takes place deep in the wilderness, in unhealthy places where many die of malaria, black-water fever, and a host of abdominal complaints. When the prospecting is complete, the balata harvest follows. The Negro worker puts on his spurs and climbs a bolletri (balata tree), slashes it open with his owru (machete), and the milk flows. The white color is always the same, but the company will later pay different rates for first, second, and third-rate balata. This work goes on from January to about August. The earnings depend on the amount of balata collected. In the future, this amount will probably decrease over time, owing to a damaging system of overharvesting, which almost seems to have been designed to exhaust this natural source of Surinamese prosperity as quickly as possible. Nowadays, the average earnings of a balata bleeder over the full eight months of the year that he works are approximately thirty guilders. The foremen or super-visors, who manage around five to eight workers each, earn about twice that much. Meanwhile, their households have almost no money, so their wives have to try to earn a little extra by cleaning houses or taking in laundry, leaving their children behind at home unsupervised. And the moral implications of husbands and wives being separated for months are easy to imagine.

Free Labor

The main reason it was necessary to import indentured coolies was that, after the ten-year period of state supervision, large numbers of former slaves took up what is called "small farming." Of course, the government could simply have accepted this fact and taken it as the point of departure for building up economic life in the colony. That would have been the natural way to lead the people to prosperity, and if they had chosen that path, Suriname would now be the supplier of horticultural products to Curaçao, since our sparsely populated country is much better suited to market gardening than to large-scale agriculture. But no one in this country thought of that. The government focused all its attention on the large companies, regarding small farmers merely as a necessary evil, taking away workers from the plantations and at best producing certain staple goods for wholesalers. On the other hand, the Surinamese were only fooling themselves if they truly believed their smallholdings would open the way to a better life. The problem is the very high tenancy fees. Right now, a small farmer who can piece together an income of three hundred guilders a year is looked up to as a wealthy man![14] Let us look at what prevents the pikin burus (small farmers) from attaining true prosperity.

First of all, they are of course highly dependent on good connections to both the city and the outside world. This is where they run into one immediate obstacle: the shipping monopoly of the Koninklijke West-Indische Maildienst (Royal West Indian Mail Service), which charges such extortionate rates that it is cheaper for the people of Curaçao to import goods from the United States or South America.[15] But connections between Suriname's agricultural areas and the country's own centers of trade are also very few and far between. The only mode of continuous transportation is water. Although Suriname does have a railroad, it runs straight to the hinterland, was built for the sole purpose of gold mining, has no connection to the South American rail network, and is completely unsuitable as a link between agricultural settlements. Furthermore, the price of rail transportation has been inflated to such unjustifiable heights in recent years, and train service has been so greatly reduced, that some places, such as the Lelydorp area, have been almost depopulated. Small farmers tend to use oxcarts and donkey carts to transport their produce, often walking more than forty kilometers along the railway tracks. The only other effects of the rise in rail fares have been a steep drop in passenger traffic and a steady decrease of the population in the first Para zone. Every district that is home to small farmers suffers the impact of these limited means of transportation. In Coronie, a district lacking even in ordinary country roads, the population decided, without any form of government support, to sell coconuts, a typical product of small-scale agriculture. In 1932, the colonial administration suddenly forbade them to ship these coconuts to the city. But more than 25,000 could not be sold on the local market, whereas in Paramaribo, they could have fetched a good price.

This same district of Coronie produces excellent livestock, and this industry could easily be expanded. The strange thing, however, is that this livestock cannot be sold, even as meat is being imported to Paramaribo from Demerara (British Guiana). The reason is that all transportation between Paramaribo and Coronie is by sea on boats that are old, worn-out, and much too small. Large vessels have to anchor for at least a couple of hours off the coast of Coronie, and their passengers and goods must be transferred on the high seas to a kind of lighter barge, at some risk to their lives. This smaller vessel can then be rowed over the wide mudbank that has formed just off the coast, a stunt that can only be pulled off at high tide. Then it must travel the entire length of a five-kilometer canal before finally reaching Coronie. Since this form of disembarkation is difficult enough in ordinary weather and almost impossible in even slightly rough seas, the goods are often seriously damaged in transit. It is not unusual for passengers to wait up to fifteen hours, in an open rowboat on the high seas, for the steamboat to arrive.

But a country road connecting Coronie to the rest of Sranan would be easy to construct, without any special feats of engineering. It would give access to an ideal region for coconut cultivation, stock and poultry farming, and vast timber operations. But the roads are lacking, just as they are elsewhere, and despite all the state commissions, there is not even an adequate plan for building any. Yet how easy it would be to make such roads in a country where calcined clay is so inexpensive and the ground is full of shell ridges! Passable roads are the first step toward the success of small farming in Suriname.

The standard of water management is also abominable. It is all very well to demand that poor colored farmers build their own dams for their smallholdings along the rivers, but how much will come of that when these farmers lack the means to do the job properly?

Part of Charlesburg and the areas on either side of the railroad to the south of Lelydorp are constantly flooded, because there is no drainage system for the large volumes of water from the swamps. The Tout-lui-fout Canal, originally built to drain these areas, is too shallow and too poorly maintained to work properly.

The small farmers in the village of Mattonshoop have lost their connecting road to overgrowth and are now completely cut off from adequate contact with the outside world. At every turn, the small farmer loses out, and rent cancellation or reduction, the only thing that could help him, is not forthcoming.

To make matters worse, the colony has no agricultural college, and the few "courses" available are obviously not enough to impart the knowledge needed to run a rational, modern agricultural business. Yet the administration continues to urge small farmers to cultivate what they call staple products, rather than encouraging a simple, profitable form of farming. No wonder the apparent success story of cocoa growing was faced with a sudden catastrophe, namely the consequences of witches' broom disease. Yet every sort of concession continues to be made to large-scale agriculture, from an exemption from medical tax (40,000 guilders) to interest-free government advances to coffee plantations and the introduction of new crop varieties for large agricultural companies, while small farmers receive no form of aid. The Hindus of Commewijne complain that the commission estimating rental value for tax purposes often sets that value at sixty guilders for a building that cost less than sixty guilders to build. Income tax assessments are sometimes based on arbitrary standards. And then there are road maintenance and landing fees. In the Colonial States, Mr. Putscher has described how a British Indian demolished his landing and waded through the mud every time instead because he could not afford the tax.

For approximately two years, there was a belief that American capital would bring a new form of agriculture to Suriname. The prospects were good, because a market was offered for the products. In the United States, a raw material for producing certain paints was in demand. The alcohol derived from the starch of the bitter cassava is reported to be exceptionally suitable for use in high-quality metallic paints.

In the second half of the year 1927, an American businessman visited Suriname with a view to obtaining the raw material for that alcohol. Yet it was not until a year later that the Netherlands devoted more thought to the idea of growing cassava in Suriname and the matter was further investigated in the colony.

Unfortunate Suriname! When it does not miss opportunities because of exaggerated optimism, it often does so because of unwarranted pessimism. Both problems are almost always due mainly to misunderstandings about the true conditions in the interior. This is how cassava growing – which is in fact the earliest form of South American agriculture – became yet another failure in Suriname.

And this is in spite of the fact that any humble schoolmaster in Berg en Dal can tell us that the small farmers in that area grow large quantities of cassava. If only the authorities had listened to the despised small farmers of Suriname, they would have obtained a different result than our thoroughly scientific institute did under its Swiss director. But whoever thinks of finding out what the little man knows? The overriding principle is that a colored person is unable to accomplish anything a white person cannot.

And when the facts contradict that principle ... well, in that case, a European expert is like the farmer who stood in front of the camel's pen and said with great confidence, "There is no such animal!"

We ourselves come from a family of small farmers. How sad our mother looked when we came home hungry and there was no cassava bread on the shelf. When we had some food in the house, our mother would cook a pot of rice, sprinkle it with herring brine, and divide it up among us to the best of her ability. We know what it means when the Outpatient Clinic Association writes, as it did on June 30, 1931, "The medical treatment received by the children is to a large extent ineffective in many cases because of their poor physical condition. There are already approximately 124 children in this category."

We know that small farmers are going through hard times. In the unemployment protest on June 17, 1931, Mr. Stuger once again made a number of demands:

1. Establishment of an agricultural council. Advice and information.
2. Exemption from rent, income tax, and rental value tax for two years.
3. Forgiveness of all agricultural debt for those financially incapable of paying back advances.
4. Free distribution of parcels of land for small farming, for a period of six years.
5. Free supply of simple agricultural tools and implements and of seeds and other plant material for a period of two years.
6. Free medical treatment, including medicine and inpatient nursing, for the first two years.
7. Support for growing one or more staple products.
8. The right to purchase a parcel of land after five years at its value prior to cultivation.
9. A special rate for farmers who transport agricultural products by public transportation.
10. Aid during the first six months, whether in cash or in provisions.
11. Free supply of materials for setting up a worker's home.

It is good that these demands have been made and that a mass of people support them. But will they ever be more than pipe dreams as long as Suriname is governed by the present regime? Only when the populace plays a genuine role in running the colony can they put an end to the current situation, in which small farmers are the daily slaves of bitter deprivation.

Free Workers

> Das Ambacht soll seinen Mann ernähren.
> As for the workers, however little they are paid for their indentured labor, they seem to make ends meet.
> *The Economic and Financial Situation in the Colony of Suriname*, p. 64[16]

Relatively few plantation workers were born in Suriname.

The memory of those sites of horror has lived on in infamy in our households. When we were children, Grandfather used to tell us, "on this plantation I was punished with the 'seven-way Spanish billy goat,' on that one your grandmother was murdered because she would not give in to the master's desires, and on that one Uncle Jantsie or Aunt Leeza was hanged," we can hardly be expected to rush enthusiastically back to the same plantation to work for sixty cents a day for men, or forty cents for women. Surinamese workers would rather go to the gold fields or the balata companies, where at least they can earn a guilder and a half to two guilders a day. "Moreover," the government report reminds us, "one must keep in mind when considering the wage figures above that the workers' wives also perform indentured labor, and the family is therefore not solely dependent on the man's earnings."

It is true: in Suriname, our women perform indentured labor and all other forms of labor besides. Otherwise there would be no way to solve the riddle of keeping a family alive in the expensive city of Paramaribo, even if just with a little rice, plantain, bread, and salted fish (or, in times of exceptional prosperity, with small portions of salted meat or bacon). The rent for a studio apartment there is eight guilders a month, and for a one or one-and-a-half bedroom apartment, twenty to twenty-five guilders a month.

Our women work as kokis, housemaids, nannies, washerwomen, and house servants, in factories, and on the plantations. Unprotected by any law, our women work for days on end for wages of eight guilders a month plus food or thirty-five guilders a month without food.

They come home drained and then do the household work for their husband and children. During the working day, those children have no parent at home to look after them.

And the children grow up.

We do not let them become indentured workers if we can avoid it. We would rather our child become a dockworker, porter, barrow-man, deliveryman, or rower along the harbor. Under the ordinance of January 23, 1899, the police commissioner decides who will be admitted to these occupations and sets the wages, which are non-negotiable. Those selected do not have the right to refuse to provide the services required of them. A dockworker's wages are two guilders a day for nine to ten hours of work, while a porter receives about three-quarters of this amount, and a rower earns only half as much for eleven to twelve hours of work. There is constant unrest because employers often do not pay even the full official amount.

Or we may find a job for our son in one of Suriname's few factories. Mechanical industry is not very far advanced here. Gas for engines costs fourteen cents per cubic meter (or twenty cents per cubic meter for individuals, a price which ensures that no working-class home will have gas or electricity). There is also a shortage of raw materials and repair shops. Wages are roughly equal to those of plantation coolies. There is no labor inspectorate. As *De Banier* has written:

> The condition and acceptability of the present arrangements receive no attention whatsoever from the authorities. There are rice mills with scorched boilers and furnaces, coffee-drying machines on farms that have not been checked, etc. Since the machines still run, work continues at full speed, without any inspection of whether the parts meet technical standards or even a test of boiler pressure. There are no professionals to service the machines; so-called machinists and mechanics never have any special training.

This is the situation throughout the country, in rice mills and in banana drying plants, in coconut oil manufacturing and in factories for carbonated drinks, in sawmills and in match factories. There is no trade union to protect the interests of industrial workers.

But in general, Suriname's young people do their best to learn some trade or other, not in order to fill their bellies (one guilder a day is a standard wage in Suriname, whether for a factory worker or for a tradesman), but because it will later enable them to emigrate abroad, where employers are eager to hire the "lazy" Surinamese, whom they know to be good employees.

But in Suriname, learning a trade is not easy. First of all, most boys come from families in such dire straits that they must start earning money as early as possible. Second, the colony does not have an extensive, well-functioning system of technical education. In Beekhuizen, the public authorities have set up a system of unpaid apprenticeships, and unfortunately, more and more private employers are following their example. As the country becomes less and less prosperous, it is increasingly common for parents to be unable to afford proper work clothes for their boys. The boys then hang around the neighborhood, getting into all kinds of trouble, and slowly but surely become ripe for the house of correction.

Once a boy has learned a trade and the time comes when he wants to start out for himself, he does not have the money to buy decent tools or a stock of materials and goods. So, at the very start of his career, he falls into the clutches of lenders, who often go on sucking the poor wretch's blood for the rest of his days. Is it any surprise, then, that in these circles too, there is grinding poverty, or that most families are perpetually in hock to some Chinese shopkeeper, who no longer even goes to the trouble of weighing their purchases but fills the bags to whatever level the barometer of his mood indicates? Is it any surprise that, in the hope of being liberated from this miserable state, people turn to the game of pyaw?

What other paths are there to choose?

In the commercial sector, at least sales clerks earn fifteen to twenty guilders a week, while office workers in large commercial enterprises receive wages of six hundred guilders a year. This explains why that type of office work is so sought after, although many whites attribute that fact to an aversion to manual labor. The claim is made repeatedly by those who have never worked with their hands, let alone for Surinamese wages.

Other young Surinamese people seek work in the public sector, even though there too, they receive unequal treatment to the fortunate employees of the same rank who hold degrees from the Netherlands. A large government apparatus obviously needs an army of officials. In practical terms, only the lowest ranks are accessible to the

Surinamese, and even for those, candidates are required to have attended the expensive Hendrikschool or St. Paulusschool ("advanced elementary education," as it is known, because there is no secondary grammar school in all Suriname!) until the age of sixteen. The children of proletarians are excluded from even the lowest rank of officials. The starting salary for this coveted official post is three hundred guilders a year. The managerial positions in the machinery of government are held by Dutch officials. These whites often receive salaries of twenty-five, fifty, or even one hundred times as much as the earnings of the Surinamese officials.

Finally, Surinamese workers play various roles in education, earning starting salaries of approximately six hundred guilders a year. Senior educational staff members, such as teachers, are generally sent from the Netherlands, and for any type of career advancement, a Surinamese employee must go to the Netherlands to obtain a degree. But the "Counselor for Students at the Ministry of the Colonies" has issued an explicit warning that the expected costs for a student at a secondary school are at least one hundred and thirty-five guilders a month, and for a university student at least one hundred and seventy-five guilders. If the costs of the voyage there and back are added to these figures, it is clear that only a few very privileged Surinamese individuals can afford the luxury of this kind of academic education for their children.

Consider the additional disadvantages of inadequate education, generally at denominational schools, of having thought in a foreign language from an early age, and of studying in a foreign climate, far from friends and family, and compare the costs with the usual Surinamese wages, and then tell us what chance a Surinamese person has to provide for himself, even to a modest standard!

In Search of Gold

It was in search of gold that the Dutch came to Suriname, and even today, the distinguished gentlemen in the colonial administration building prick up their ears when they hear the jingle of that precious metal. This tantalizing music was first heard during the administration of Jonkheer Cornelis Ascanius van Sypesteyn, and it seemed that a centuries-long dream was about to come true. A few bold pioneers, while passing through the forests of a mountainous region, had found gold in the creeks, and soon thousands of hectares were being designated by the colonial government as mining concessions. It truly seemed as if the highest expectations would be fulfilled; it was not unusual to find gold nuggets seven and a half kilograms in weight, and in just twenty years, the colony exported more than twenty-three million guilders' worth of gold.

This short-lived mania, soon brought to an end by completely haphazard overexploitation, gave Suriname its well-known railroad. After three years of heavy labor in the colony, Jonkheer Van Asch van Wijk went on leave in the Netherlands on May 13, 1894. After he requested his permanent discharge in 1895, the deputy governor, former colonial secretary Warmolt Tonckens, was appointed first as his substitute and, in 1896, as the next governor. He attached importance to the interests of the large syndicates formed around that time to focus energy and resources on extracting Suriname's gold. These syndicates were clamoring for better transportation connections, so in July 1897 a private company called the Maatschappij Suriname was granted the right to construct and operate a tram line from Paramaribo to the Lawa area. This company clearly had no trouble obtaining a variety of grants and privileges from the administration. The matter was addressed with unusual speed, and not long afterwards, in January 1898, a commission of Dutch engineers and geologists came to Suriname to begin work on the railroad, under the supervision of the engineer Grinwis Plaat. Now, a railroad is generally built to create a link between countries, or between different villages, plantations, or farms in the same country. The railroad in Suriname, however, for which the wooden ties were ordered from abroad, makes a beeline for the gold in the wilderness. Its route runs south from Paramaribo to the primeval forest. By the time it had been completed, it was clear that gold exploitation in that region was no longer profitable.

The gold fields themselves still afford a meager living to a number of coolies, who earn wages of around one and a half guilders a day for their work in one of Suriname's unhealthiest areas.

The Major Crops

If gold could not be conjured straight out of the ground, it was hoped that at least large-scale agriculture could make Suriname's river of gold flow again. Little large-scale sugar production now remains. Since the abolition of slavery, the whites no longer care for that sort of business, and out of eighty-five plantations, only five remain in operation. Even so, production remains fairly high, since improved agricultural methods and machinery have greatly increased productivity per hectare. The total yield was 6.5 million kilograms a year in 1700 and 10.5 million in 1760. This shows that, since the abolition of slavery, production per worker has skyrocketed. These businesses could undoubtedly charge better prices for their products if each factory did not have to specialize in one particular variety of molasses, an approach that makes it impossible to sell anything approaching mass quantities.

Alongside sugar, coffee was one of Suriname's leading export commodities. The original variety grown there was Arabica, which is still the greatest commercial success in neighboring Brazil. The disadvantage of this type of coffee, however, is that not all the beans are ripe at the same time, so the harvest requires many people to be at work for a long while. Paying all those workers was the last thing the plantation owners wanted to do. As late as the eighteenth century, Suriname's annual coffee production was still fifteen million kilograms. After slavery was abolished, however, the coffee production area dwindled from 258 hectares in 1862 to 78 in 1873. Then someone had the bright idea of planting Liberia coffee, so that all the beans would ripen at the same time and less labor (and therefore less pay) would be required. In 1903–1904, 91 hectares were planted with this crop, and the total yield was 269,218 kilograms. But when the price of Liberia coffee dropped to 33.5 cents per kilogram, the berries were left on the trees, fields in the midst of cultivation were razed, and cocoa was planted there.

Cocoa cultivation soon expanded in Suriname, with plantations shooting up like mushrooms and vanishing again just as fast. In 1862, cocoa production area totaled 593 hectares. By 1873, this figure had risen to 1,913 hectares. In 1904, more than 7,000 of the 10,229 hectares used for large-scale agriculture were planted with cocoa. The welfare of small farmers was partly dependent on this cocoa cultivation. Then witches' broom disease struck the cocoa trees, and by 1904 total yields had dropped to a quarter of their former level: from ƒ 2,837,000 guilders in 1893 to ƒ 538,000 in 1904. It has still not proven possible to bring this crop disease under control in Suriname.

To make the wellspring of Surinamese dividends flow once more, our country was equipped with an agricultural research station, where a number of technicians, flagrantly neglecting the interests of small farmers, are searching for the philosopher's stone for large-scale agriculture. Many a thorny question could be raised about this expensive institute, but let us simply refer to the great expert Mr. L. Junker's observation about cassava cultivation in the *West-Indische Gids* in May 1931:

> As always, the fundamental error lies in the fact that those who grew up in this country and are native to it are not given the opportunity for further development, while business is done by people who at best have become familiar with our country after long years spent here, but who will in any case always remain foreigners, and whose priority is to serve foreign interests.

What Becomes of those Millions?

> And I dare to tell you merchants, you Sunday Christians: this is *your* fault. Having taken possession of this country – I will not speak of justice or injustice, only God can judge that – why have you ceased to love it, now that it no longer brings you a Dividend? These days, you recognize this country only as a loss in your annual accounts and a grating reminder of the fat years of Mauricius and Van Sommelsdijk. You schemingly calculate how many tax-free years the sale of this country could give you. Suriname was once your sugar land, was it not? This is the way you sell a slave, the way you sell a crippled child. And in your high-stooped house along the green city canal, or in your stately country home by the Vecht River or on a lake, you have no idea in what solitude the banished children of this country wander the earth; your daughter at her romantic piano has no idea that my Hawaii is shriveling under the hot sun.
>
> Albert Helman

Three million guilders is the annual contribution of the mother country to Suriname's budget deficit. Three million

– that's a lot of money, isn't it? It may even be the average income of one of your esteemed Dutch millionaires. Three million is how much is lost on the stock market on a bad day in an economic crisis. Three million ... What in the name of the Lord are those lazy niggers doing with our three million magnificent gold-standard guilders?

Yes, what does become of those millions? No, gentlemen, I assure you they do not end up in my mother's pocket; long before the week is out, she is taking a hard look at her last penny. And they're not in the pockets of our hundreds of unemployed workers, as our support committee in Suriname holds to the firm principle that "financial support to the unemployed inevitably has a demoralizing effect."

They aren't in the hospitals, or the universities, or the charities.

"Did you know," *De Banier* wrote on July 3, 1931, "that the Portuguese government has strictly forbidden public begging? Or that, in contrast, Suriname encourages it, in order to avoid the expense of public poor relief?"

No, you cannot complain that in Suriname your millions are thrown away on ethical vagaries, arts, sciences, or other superfluous luxuries of that kind. Your millions, insofar as they do not go toward the extremely high salaries of the colonial administrators, contribute to the immense sums wasted on creating promising new opportunities in which Suriname's major planters can invest their capital.

Come, we will tell you a multi-million-guilder fairy tale. A tale of two crops: the Pará rubber tree and the banana.

The Pará Rubber Tree
Why did Suriname's planters take up the Pará rubber tree? As always under capitalism, they were dazzled by a short-lived boom, by the exceptional profit margin that rubber cultivation momentarily seemed to offer them. If they had not fallen under the spell of this rubber "tree," then surely no one would ever have dreamed that this

particular plant, which requires so much labor and such meticulous care, was the crop to import into our sparsely populated country. But once the planters began to dream of glittering gold, they could not wait to try the experiment, although the plutocrats were prudent enough to make the government pay for it. This is how it came about that, in 1908, the colonial administration began operating the rubber plantation Slootwijk. The same people who are normally such bitter opponents of state enterprises suddenly admired the government's initiative as soon as it started relieving their balance sheets of the risk of private initiative (that much-praised thing).

> This enterprise, founded in accordance with a decision made in 1908, has no other objective than to earn a profit from rubber planting for the colonial administration. In the light of that fact, its location on the Commetewane, very far from Paramaribo, which would probably not be advantageous under any circumstances, would be completely unsuitable if, as one might have recommended, the enterprise had been regarded as a large-scale experiment to be judged not primarily by its financial results but by the lessons it could teach the planters. (Report of the Commission appointed by Royal Decree of the Ministry of Colonies, March 11, 1911, pp. 29 and 39)

Here again we find the usual short-sighted drive for profit that dooms the attempt to failure from the start. In spite of that, and against the advice of government specialists, money is still being thrown away on additional planting on the same site. It has become a matter of prestige, and the coolies are being pushed to the limit so that the result will at least be presentable. In the meantime, the rubber boom has long since deflated, and everywhere else in the world production was restricted some time ago. We have no reason to praise the foresight or discernment of our colony's leaders!

The Banana Debacle

Axiom: Suriname costs the Netherlands millions, and the Negro is lazy.

This story begins with the dismaying discovery that our attempts at cocoa cultivation had failed completely. The total export value dropped from 2.3 million in 1901 to 1.4 million in 1903 and then to 500,000 guilders in 1904. So our colonial administrators put their heads together to find a new product for large-scale agriculture. Governor Lely thought he had hit upon the answer: bananas.

They relied mainly on material about banana cultivation in Jamaica. The agricultural inspector, Dr. Van Hall, reviewed the literature and may have obtained additional information in writing; *at the time, however, he himself did not visit any countries where bananas were cultivated.* The *association for large-scale agriculture* did, however, send a planter to Jamaica with financial support from the colony to learn about banana cultivation and export and gather the information needed for introducing this crop to Suriname. This planter's *unpublished report, which did not impress our commission as being thorough,* was the foundation, along with the aforementioned written information, on which a whole new form of cultivation, which would cost the colonial coffers three-quarters of a million, was brought into being.[17]

The possibility of disease seems never to have occurred to them (in Suriname, there is a rumor that bribery by the United Fruit Company led to the purchase of bad seed!); it was thought that success was guaranteed simply because a plant somewhat similar to the chosen crop was indigenous to Suriname and because the type of banana needed for export, the Gros Michel variety, was not susceptible to disease in Jamaica. They seem not to have given any thought to the fact that it is a quite different thing, whether here or there, to grow a type of banana for local use than it is to carry out the large-scale transplantation of an export variety that has been grown elsewhere for years and which will be held to high standards. It stands to reason that while planters and workers in Jamaica and elsewhere had gained expert knowledge of this crop over time, knowledge that could not be acquired from one day to the next in Suriname.

Knowledge, for instance, of how long it will take for forests to reach maturity, so that the vast majority of trees will be ready for shipping in the months when the best price can be negotiated. This art, which is fundamental to obtaining the high average price that the Surinamese plans depended on, had been mastered by Jamaica's planters only through long experience.

After this poor preparation, the governor submitted a bill to the Colonial States "regarding the introduction of banana cultivation for export." The state, like a loving father, proposed to extend a helping hand to the poor planters, thereby ushering in radiant prosperity for both parties. Forty plantations were to plant seventy-five hectares each within three years, using their own coolies but following the government's instructions. In return, they were to receive a government advance of 560 guilders per hectare at four percent interest. If they made a profit on the crop, they were allowed to keep it; if they incurred a loss, they had to pay back the difference in ten interest-free annual installments. It was assumed that the revenue from the harvest of this first series would cover the costs of planting series 2 and 3; the costs of planting three hundred hectares were therefore estimated at ƒ 750,000.

Of course, this scheme was expected to bring the profits rolling in. Governor Lely calculated that even in the first few years, it was safe to assume exports of 650 bunches per hectare, yielding around ƒ 420 in revenue. The estimated costs were *f* 360 per hectare for the first year and *f* 180 for each subsequent year. This implies a profit of *f* 60 per hectare in the first year, rising to *f* 240 per hectare in the next.

The ordinance was passed by the States on July 22, 1905. Since it called for 3,000 hectares of land to be planted with bananas, Minister Dirk Fock submitted a bill to increase the relevant item in the budget for Suriname by *f* 270,000. This became law on December 30, 1905.

The United Fruit Company (UFCO) had already established a monopoly on sales throughout North America, the most promising region for the sale of Surinamese bananas.[18] No one thought of breaking this monopoly. For instance, the Royal Dutch West India Mail could have offered low rates. But the responsible authorities were only too happy to shift the risk involved in sales onto someone else's shoulders. So the United Fruit Company was chosen to sell the product, even though the price they offered was much lower than had been expected and counted on.

By this time, Governor Idenburg had taken office. To his dismay, he discovered that the planters were not nearly as tempted by the government's offer as had been hoped. In fact, it proved impossible to persuade enough of them to sign up for the remaining 2,500 hectares in 75-hectare parcels. So the authorities settled for an alternative: a number of neglected plantations, which had gone partly or completely uncultivated for many years, signed up for 140 to 375 hectares. To obtain even this outcome, the Surinamese government and the Ministry of Colonies had to put the planters and their Dutch financiers under pressure.

See p. 144 of the aforementioned commission's report: "No sooner had the 3,000 hectares been fully subscribed, with great difficulty, on August 1, 1906, than the contract with the Fruit Company, which was by then already showing signs of impatience, was signed. But that same month, requests arrived from plantations to reduce their subscription. The handling of the whole affair was riddled with mistakes, which, as one might expect, had grave repercussions in later years."

By obtaining subscriptions under duress, Mother Holland had not only assumed a heavy moral burden but also put the whole plan on shaky foundations. On the assumption that almost every plantation would sign up for 75 hectares, the project was not too risky. The new crop would provide work for the coolies no longer needed in the cocoa fields and, more importantly, "the vast sums poured into housing for immigrants etc. would lead to financial returns." If banana growing yielded large profits after three years, it would help the plantations; but if the plan failed, then at least not much banana would have been planted relative to other crops, and the debt could be paid off in ten installments. But the situation was very different once two-thirds of the total area supported by the colonial administration was on only eight plantations, which had planted 1,782 hectares with bananas and only 668 hectares with coffee, cocoa, or rubber trees.

Let us return to the commission's remarks:

> Even minor cost overruns would therefore compel the government to exceed its stated maximum of *f* 360 if it wished to ensure the continued viability of the business, *which was the government's only form of collateral for its loan.* And if the crop failed completely, then of course none of the money advanced to these plantations could be recovered. (p. 145)

The contract with the Fruit Company was based on three hundred hectares of banana cultivation, and if the colonial administration supplied too little, it would have to pay a fine, which it hoped to pass on to the plantation owners by paying a lower price per bunch of bananas. But the

most astonishing thing of all was that the United Fruit
Company, which had an adequate supply of bananas
from other countries, was actually hoping to receive the
fine instead of the fruit. And it was that very company
that took the noble step of sending G.H. Williams, of its
agriculture department, to advise and assist the planters.
So we should not be too surprised to read in the commission's later report "that in view of Suriname's particular
soil conditions, some of Williams's recommendations were
unfortunate"!

According to a paper from the colony's financial administrator, C.A.J. Struycken de Roysancour:

> While the original plan had assumed a price of *f* 0.90
> per full bunch, a price of *f* 0.87½ was negotiated with
> the United Fruit Company only for the best months, and
> prices of *f* 0.75 and *f* 0.50 for the rest of the year. As
> attempts to influence ripening time had no discernible
> effect, the average price was no more than *f* 0.61.
> Furthermore, the first bananas were harvested not after
> a year, as expected, but seventeen or eighteen months
> after the operation began. That made it necessary, after
> paying out the establishment costs over a period of four
> months, to provide another thirteen to fourteen months
> of operating expenses, at an annual rate of *f* 180, before
> the first harvest.

The funds allocated for operating expenses proved
insufficient. The demanding conditions imposed on the
plantations required them to pay the travel costs and
taxes for bringing immigrant workers into the country,
so they had to be lent additional money for that purpose.
In other words, the state paid its own taxes. Do you see
now, readers, what becomes of your millions? Maximum
support for operating costs was increased from *f* 180 to
f 276. In short, the costs kept increasing and the benefits
kept dwindling, and at this stage, to make the catastrophe

complete, the bananas fell prey to a plant disease: Panama disease.

The colonial administration, which was morally responsible for the success of the banana crop, soon had no choice but to increase the advances to the planters, who claimed to have run out of operating capital. This increased their debt burden to such heights that many of them rushed to convert their businesses into limited liability companies, so that only the plantation itself would be counted as collateral. And after the administration had allowed them to do so, it soon transpired that many plantations had debts greater than their value – so much greater that even the recovery of the banana crop would not solve the problem.

From this point onward, the directors of the limited liability companies no longer had any incentive to limit their debt. The salaries of the managers and the representatives in Paramaribo sometimes rose to incredible heights, and the report informs us that "it has even been known to happen that profits from other crops were paid out as dividends. Once it became clear that the colonial administration believed it had no way of stopping this, there was an obvious incentive to use funds provided for banana cultivation for other crops instead" (p. 149).

The result was the use of the government support for personal gain. The report refers to "the possibility of dishonest practices" and adds that "egregious examples can be given." Only at this stage did the agriculture department begin to audit expense statements; this resulted in the swift dismissal of a number of plantation administrators and even in the placement of some plantations in receivership.

The Gros Michel banana experiment was an utter failure.

Then a plan was made to try the Congo variety. The idea was to plant 2,798 hectares with a combination of coffee and bananas. After two years, these two crops would begin to interfere with one another, and a decision could be made about which of the two to chop down. A peculiar experiment. This was going too far for the minister, so the Dutch parliament decided in February 1911 to liquidate the entire banana cultivation project, budgeting 500,000 guilders for this purpose.[19]

By late 1907, all but 100,000 guilders of this budget had been spent, and by 1908 the budget had been far exceeded. Yet in 1909, Governor Pieter Hofstede Crull and the minister of the colonies, A.W.F. Idenburg, included not a word about the affair in their explanatory memorandum to the budget. By 1908, spending on the project had exceeded revenue by 1,100,000, without anyone raising the alarm. It was 1910 by the time Governor Dirk Fock's explanatory memorandum to the budget made tentative mention of "a few setbacks." But where are the figures? Nowhere to be found, all swallowed up in accordance with the axiom: Suriname costs the Netherlands millions, and the Negro is lazy.

In truth, it would have been difficult to produce figures, because when the lower house of the Dutch parliament asked "whether commercial accounting methods had been adopted so that good projections could be made of the financial results," the only possible answer was that, to put it mildly, no commercial accounts could be submitted, because the figures were missing.

It was not until 1911 that the colony's financial administration published a paper about the banana cultivation affair, and the Dutch finance minister declared, with emphasis, that it was the first time *since 1905* that he had been given a clear picture of the course of events. How can they talk of the benefits of the mother country supervising its child, the colony, when they do not notice anything is wrong until the original estimate of f 750,000 has been exceeded by two million?!

The Liquidation of the Banana Debacle

> All this gives reason for optimism that banana growing will
> eventually be a boon to the colony and reward all the work
> that a series of governors and their officials have devoted to
> this form of agriculture.[20]

Banana growing in Suriname reminds us very much of the
honest angler who says to his friend, "Boy, you should
have seen the size of the pike I caught!", and then, a while
later, adds, "But it fell back into the water."

As of January 15, 1911, the support was reduced to the
average yield per hectare per month over the most recent
time period, but planters who desired additional funding
could receive the earlier amount of twenty-three guilders
a month (*f* 276 a year) for each hectare still under cultivation. As for the United Fruit Company, it was discovered
to object to the dissolution of the contract concluded
with it.

The governor drafted a bill giving him the authority to
take any measures he deemed necessary with regard to
banana debt as of January 1, 1911, *including partial or total
debt cancellation*, to the end of enabling the plantations
to go on cultivating the fields planted with bananas and,
if possible, even to enlarge the area under cultivation. The
governor could also replace the original collateral mortgage
with other forms of security or relinquish it, temporarily or
permanently. The intention was to make the plantations pay
their entire debt to the government, but to reduce that debt
by awarding bonuses for continuing to cultivate the fields
planted with bananas.[21] The maximum debt reduction was
set at 75 percent, but if the cultivated area was expanded,
the remainder of the debt could also be forgiven.

Generosity to large agricultural companies. Stinginess
toward the Surinamese workers, who were exploited on
the banana plantations.

This system, too, collapsed like a house of cards and, soon enough, the debts to the colonial regime were also found to be worthless, because mortgages had been issued in connection with fictitious debt. You see, to enable plantations to acquire new capital, the government had, by ordinance of March 7, 1911, made its own collateral mortgage for banana planters a non-priority debt. In the end, the authorities developed yet another new system, under which a mortgage claim on the banana plantations could be converted into a ground rent. This made it possible for the plantations to apply for still more credit.

Now that the horse has bolted, the stable door is shut, and the millions have well and truly vanished, twenty-five years after the start of banana cultivation, the authorities have arrived at a surprising insight.

They have now discovered:

- that banana growing is not by any means as straight-forward as they had first thought; on the contrary, the appropriate tillage method and plantation layout depend on the type of soil and on whether multiple cropping takes place;
- that the last series of Gros Michel planted has defied expectations by holding up much better (now that the United Fruit Company is no longer involved!);
- that the Congo variety may be more resistant to Panama disease but has a very questionable market value;
- that the Chinese banana variety once seen in Sranan as unsuitable for export has become a very popular commodity;
- and that, in conclusion, a feel for the market is essential, because as the product continues to reach new areas and new social circles, the prices are in constant flux.

So now the real experimentation has just begun. The agricultural research station intends to plant a wide range of varieties, and very learned commissions are on their way abroad. And why shouldn't they? The funds are available, and the honoraria have reached the level of the Srananliba at high tide. Even though, after all these years, banana cultivation is still in an early stage of development, there is no need to give up hope that one day the spring of gold will begin to flow and the owners of large agricultural companies will then be able to join the ranks of Dutch millionaires. This is how the millions intended for Suriname benefit a small clique of capitalists, while the vast majority of people live in poverty. And Dutch schoolchildren still learn the axiom: The Negro is lazy, and Suriname costs us millions![22]

Results

> *Wroko di furu, ma wrokoman mankeri.*
> *Work aplenty, but workers are lacking.*[23]

In the long procession that winds through the streets of Paramaribo on the morning of Wednesday, June 17, 1931, many people wear small red flags with the slogan, "GIVE US WORK, 5,000 FAMILIES ARE IN NEED, HELP, HELP, HELP!"

Five thousand families are in need. This time, it is not the kind of need to which Surinamese families are accustomed, the kind of need that has become almost a habit. No, what they mean this time is the most urgent need of all: famine, the need that sends a father out onto the road with his eight children, walking forty kilometers because he has no money for the journey but nonetheless hopes to find help in Paramaribo. Five thousand families are in need, not including the Javanese families who are turned away when they apply for jobs and end up falling into crime, and not including the thousands of Surinamese in Curaçao and around the world who are double victims of their foreign nationality and of the depression.

Five thousand families are in need. Help, help, help!

And the bourgeoisie rushes to their aid.

The Kino Theater in Bellevue donates the full proceeds of a screening to the unemployed. In Thalia, an evening of cabaret with Johannes Kruisland is organized to benefit the unemployed. A Surinamese aid committee is formed, and we read:

> The committee will not, however, be responsible for the creation or direct expansion of employment. That is the task of Government. Unemployment has created dire problems for many families; many children are undernourished. The committee is therefore considering how to help them, but it has no intention of taking on the task of poor relief. That is a task for other parties: the churches and Government. The committee will attempt to help undernourished school-children to obtain a daily meal, but as a matter of principle, it will reject any application for financial support for basic needs. That type of charity is generally regarded as inefficient, doing society and the individual greater harm than good. (July 5)

Such philanthropy, such good will, and yet the need grows more pressing by the day. The unemployed begin to protest. They flood the streets and are addressed by the social democrat Louis Doedel, an exile from Curaçao. It is a friendly speech, full of faith in the powers that be. "Violence is not the first means that must be used to achieve one's objectives. Always remember the proverb, 'A well-chosen word will make itself heard.' After the step you took on Wednesday, you must wait patiently to see the results you hope for. You won't see them today or tomorrow; it will take time, because the governor has to consult with the councilors and come up with a feasible plan. So you, for your part, will have to show a little patience. I urge you with all my heart to keep silent, and not to make any brash declarations incompatible with the dignity of your protest." His Excellency is asked to take the following points into careful consideration:

1. The establishment of an employment office by the colonial administration.
2. The abolition of the practice of appointing retirees to positions that open up in the administration.
3. The creation of relief work programs in which unemployed people can be employed in rotation.
4. The allocation of a few thousand hectares of land to unemployed people for mineral extraction, as well as for agricultural purposes, and government support and advice to these people for a period of three months.
5. In connection with item 4, free transportation on government vehicles to and from their place of work.
6. The supply of free food to undernourished school-children, on the same basis as in the war years.
7. The organization of a public prize lottery, the profits from which should be used to pay the interest and principal for the support to the unemployed.

Then Louis Doedel ends his speech with these well-meaning words:

> That is why we believed it necessary to approach Your Excellency, in the hope that we can be of some service to Your Excellency, as far as our feeble powers permit, in the search for ways of providing support. May Your Excellency's work in the interest of the Surinamese unemployed then bear fruit, as we all hope it will, resulting in the greater flourishing of this Territory of the Netherlands and in closer ties between the Netherlands and Suriname. And

finally, may your Excellency's efforts be borne up by the words of the Gospels: "Whatever you did for the least of My children, you did for Me."

"Thank you."

Governor Rutgers agrees to consider taking measures. And the unemployed demonstrators sing first Troelstra's song and then the Wilhelmus.[24] But on June 26, a large advertisement appears in *De Banier*:

Unemployed people of Suriname!
Do you know your governor's true nature?
Then reserve the optimism
that you have felt since your audience on Wednesday of last week.
Our mood is pessimistic, and for now will remain so!
While Rome deliberates, Saguntum is lost.[25]
Politically minded unemployed workers.

So we find destruction and cutbacks by government in every area where only construction and initiative could rescue the population from their ongoing plummet into penury! When the public sector set the example of fighting unemployment by laying off employees, private employers were naturally quick to follow. Hundreds of workers were dismissed from the Moengo mines (July 14, 1931); many of them, after six years of faithful service to their employer, were tossed out into the street with twelve days' wages.

Meanwhile, nothing is being done to alleviate the people's needs. Chinese shopkeepers no longer extend credit. Although the price of a sack of flour has fallen from ƒ 45 to ƒ 17.50, this does not seem to affect the price of bread, and when the unemployment committee invites the bakers to a meeting to discuss the possibility of lowering the bread price, those shopkeepers are conspicuous by their absence. And what is true of bread is equally true of other foods. Vacuum pan sugar costs a good deal more in Suriname than it brings on the export market. At the same time, however, a new tax on keeping chickens, ducks, geese, turkeys, pigs, goats, cows, cats, parrots, and canaries is under consideration and, with surcharges, will rake in more than a million a year. And the government runs large newspaper advertisements warning that those who do not pay their taxes in time will be fined up to three hundred guilders.

That is how utterly miserable, how exceptionally bad the situation was at that moment in the colony of Suriname. These results of centuries of colonization must give us pause.

The demonstrations by unemployed people on Red Tuesday in 1931 ended with the police firing on the protesters and attacking them with sabers, leaving one dead and many wounded.

The year is 1802; we are aboard the Pluto, *a ship of the revolutionary Batavian Republic. The boatswain's whistle sounds on deck, and when the men have fallen into formation, the captain makes a speech:*

"As you know, men, this is the age of liberty, equality, and fraternity."

"Yes, captain!"

"The topgallant needs to be taken in, but of course you don't have to do it if you're not in the mood, in this age of liberty, equality, and fraternity."

"Yes, captain!"

"But if you're not up in the mast in two minutes, I'll flog you till the twigs fly from your ribs."

"Yes, captain!"

The boatswain's whistle sounds again, the Jack Tars scurry off into the rigging, and five minutes later the sails have been taken in.

And you, Surinamese compatriots, are you familiar with freedom, equality, and fraternity?

Oh, we could have made this book much longer and heavier. There's no end to colonial chaos; we could go on to the waterworks question, the deplorable state of medical care, the lack of education, the madness of racism, and a thousand other grievances.

We will not.

We aim to show just one thing: colored compatriots, thou once wert slaves, and thou shalt go on living in poverty and misery as long as thou dost not put thy faith in thine own proletarian unity. A smallholding here or there and a shovel or a plow on credit will not help us.

We need a great plan of national reconstruction, a plan that includes collective corporations with modern equipment, owned by the workers of Suriname.

Our nation's prosperity must be built with our own hands.

This plan requires the utmost effort from us, the Surinamese. But first, our country's proletarians must develop class consciousness and a spirit of struggle; having thrown off their old slave chains, they must now throw off the old slave mentality.

Reunion and Farewell

Sranan, my fatherland, I have seen you again, and you were as beautiful as I often dreamed while tossing and turning with longing in my bed in Holland.

Over the deep blue waters of the ocean, the *Rensselaer* carries me to your coast. Flying fish, like dancing diamonds, startled by the approaching boat, fly five to six meters ahead and then dive back into the water, leaving a silvery track across its surface. The air is fresh and moist; a strong trade wind blows like a breath of freedom. Like the monotonous sound of the seagulls, my heart sings with longing for the reunion ahead.

A few blasts of the steam whistle summon us to today's boat drill. We come on deck and are told there are not enough life vests for the children. A rude awakening: you're still a prole. Below, in first class, the passengers and officers are splashing about in their swimming pool. Crew members don't count. Prole children can drown.

High in the stays and shrouds of the *Rensselaer* blows the wind of freedom. On the deck below me, a stoker emerges – white, but blacker than I am with soot from his fire – and hurries toward his stuffy quarters. Halfway along the forecastle, he waves at me and the children. In the black of his face, the whites of his eyes and his pearly teeth are smiling. That too is the same everywhere, and beautiful everywhere: the fellowship among proletarians and their love of liberty.

I am standing on the deck of the *Rensselaer* on a fine bright morning in January. Two hours ago, the sun rose from its lair with a blood-red smile; now it rolls across the spotless blue sky like a glowing cannonball, a fiery balloon, dispelling the milky veils of mist to reveal the green wall of the shoreline. Light and heat stream down from the sky to the gleaming white deck. The earth and sea of Suriname are showered in sunlight. Surging and frothing, the mighty current of the river rushes toward us. This close to the city, its water is light blue and transparent to great depths. In the forest along the bank, from which the scent of flowering mahogany trees and fresh-burnt wood are rising, an early rooster has roused all the other birds. Tyon-tyons (mangrove herons) sing their unvarying song; a water bird suddenly plunges its beak into the river and resurfaces with a fish, leaving two long ripples behind it. High in the sky circles the tingi fowru (vulture) with its grim plumage, Suriname's volunteer trash collector. The trade wind clambers like a quick brown monkey through the light green treetops, around which the morning's last dreams are still drifting. The strains of one small, blood-red songbird rise above the chorus of the other birds. Slender sailboats with white sails come down the river, alongside rowboats bright with red lead paint, the water dripping from their oars like a glittering curtain of pearls. The ship is surrounded by puffing steamboats reminiscent of water beetles and by dugouts that dart across the water like swift snakes. A shot is fired from Fort Zeelandia and echoes from the forests; a thin cloud of smoke lingers over the cannon's mouth. In her strong arms, the laughing river carries our ship to the quay. She reminds me of my father in the old days, when he carried me and my little sister high on his shoulders to market.

Among the thousand-headed crowd that awaits us on shore, my father is a feeble old man. My mother, for whom I returned, is not to be found here; she died two days after we left Holland. The whistling tune of sorrow in my heart is drowned out by the cheers that greet me. The workers of Suriname have put on their Sunday best, as if for a festival. Among the tall figures of the men, the kotomisis swirl like happy, colorful butterflies. One thousand loyal eyes blink. A hundred strong hands squeeze mine. "Na wan bigi man!" (He's an important man!), a dockworker says with a laugh. "The governor has provided him with an escort." Only now do I notice I am being followed by several detectives. In the holsters on their hips, they are carrying loaded revolvers.[1] Hoffman's drops must be a popular drink among whites in the colony these days![2] After they and they alone generated this interest in my arrival, with their hysterical fear-mongering about "the coming Messiah," now their hearts race when they imagine the potential consequences. How is it possible that the arrival of a "communist" so terrifies many of the colony's civilian and military leaders?[3] The only possible explanation is this: they know the lumber of misery is heaped so high that a single spark will set the whole pile aflame![4] Yet how could a single man threaten the entire power structure of the colony of Suriname, even if he wanted to?

In the evening, after the last visitors have left, I reflect on all the misery. Outside I hear the soft rustle of the sinsins. A bright fayaworon dances in front of the open window. In the distance a dog barks, vigilant. The moon smiles her silent smile above the treetops. The air is filled with the scent of honeysuckle. Bats, black as ink, plant hungry kisses on the ripe fruit. To the tones of hot jazz (Negroes are generous enough to entertain their masters with high-spirited music), many wealthy whites are drowning their sorrows. Here in the "filthy district," where the proletarians live, it is quiet and dark. In the cramped darkness of their four-by-four-meter houses, the colored families await the morning, sleeping heavily in their exhaustion. Not everyone is lucky enough to pass the night under a roof. These days, many sleep under bridges or on the stoops of houses. It comes back to me now how thin and sunken many faces were back at the docks, beneath their deceptive masks of joy. With a loud shriek, a startled owru kuku takes off from a tree.

In the still of the night comes a knocking at the windows. It's the detectives; they want to make sure I'm at home. It's as though someone has suddenly knocked at my heart: What will you do to ease your people's suffering? In the velvet darkness of the night I hear soft steps.

Mother, what can I do to help? My comrades are waiting. I have only just returned. So much has changed.

It seems as if my mother leans in to kiss me, the way she did when I was little, the way she listened to my complaints and my sorrow ebbed away because someone was willing to listen.

And all at once I know: I will open an advisory agency and listen to the complaints of my fellows, the same way my mother once listened to her son's sorrows. And maybe I will find a way to make them feel some fraction of the hope and courage contained in that one powerful word I learned in a foreign country: organization. Maybe I can put an end to some of the dissension that has been the weakness of these colored people; maybe it will not prove completely impossible to make Negroes, Hindustanis, Javanese, and Indians understand that only solidarity can unite all the sons of Mother Sranan in their struggle to live with dignity.

A lecture I planned to give about Surinamese history, a first attempt on my part to combat my compatriots' deep-seated inferiority complex, was made impossible, in spite of the freedom of assembly guaranteed by law, when the government denied us access to a lecture hall.[5] One venue after another closed its doors to us under pressure from higher up, and a meeting on Knijpe's property was banned by the police without any legal justification. Now every morning around five or six, I hear the bare feet of hundreds of my comrades treading down Pontenwerfstraat to our yard, where they wait patiently for hours in the shade of the big manya tree.

All around them, on the dirty corner, life is waking up. The women, taking baskitas full of bananas and manyas to market, hurry past the wooden shacks full of holes, with their truli roofs that let in water like a sieve in the rainy season. Children with swollen bellies, bowlegged from malnutrition, dysentery, and other diseases, are playing in the puddles of the sewerless, unpaved streets or beside the wells and the stinking latrines outside the houses. A vulture drags the carcass of a rat out of one of the clogged, fetid gutters. Only nature seems undisturbed by this display of misery. The birds, as cheerful as ever, rendezvous in the manya tree: the beautifully marked grikibis, the sky-blue blawforkis, and the sparrow-colored gadofowrus. Altos and basses give concerts in the sunlight, their feathers sparkling amid the grass and the klarun.

But under the tree, past my table, files a parade of misery. Pariahs with deep, sunken cheeks. Starving people. People with no resistance to disease. Open books in which to read the story, haltingly told, of oppression and deprivation. Indians, maroons, creoles, British Indians, Javanese ... some days, while the police motor squads pass in the street outside, more than fifteen hundred people come to my table. Some have traveled seven or eight days to speak to me.

One Hindu says to me, bitterly, "I have a donkey and a cart. If ever my animal has a wound, the very next moment a few policemen show up to fine me. When I had a wound on my own leg and went to the hospital to ask for free assistance, I was literally thrown out. And yet the leaders of Bharat Uday say the colonial regime means to care for us as a mother cares for her child."[6]

British Indians tell me that when they tried to file complaints, they were sent away with jeers and cries of "Wait for your Gandhi!" They can no longer afford the rental value tax on their smallholdings and the hovels built on them. Soldiers break into their houses to collect the taxes and sell the roof over their heads, the chickens in their yard, and the small supply of rice for feeding the family. The commander who determines the value of the sale is both the seller and the buyer. Then the soldiers go to the house of a family with no tax debt. Because the man of the house is not at home, his wife refuses to let the soldiers in. Although pregnant, she is flung out of the way and later gives birth to a deformed boy.

I hear the same complaints from the small farmers of Nickerie. The work in the fields there is exceptionally demanding, while the depression has driven the price of rice to rock bottom. They too can no longer pay their taxes, and they too are being driven out of their homes.

The white paper of my notebooks (which later, after my house is searched and I am arrested, will turn out to have vanished without a trace) fills with grievances.

Every district of Suriname is teeming with malaria sufferers. Most of them are as good as dead, because they have run out of money to buy quinine. A colored woman who had been in an accident died in the hospital in excruciating pain, while inquiries were in progress in her neighborhood regarding her family's ability to pay for the operation. A worker had to pawn his jacket, and a woman her bracelets, so that they could pay the doctor in Lelydorp. Tuberculosis has been a full-scale massacre. And in the year 1932 alone, there were more than 2,000 new cases of yaws!

Suriname is the land of flowers. Like the fayalobi, the flower of burning love that young lovers give each other, the red wounds bloom on her black body. Like the angalampu, the red lamp of misery hangs in front of the houses of the poor. Among the flourishing, fragrant p'pokaitongos, filiarisis, and leprosy flourish too. Where the moss gives off its scent under the palms, a young mother lies in agonizing labor for four days and dies on the fifth, along with her child. The forest boasts flowers but not a single midwife. Deep in the interior, in marshes of ice-cold water where the sun never shines, grows the colossal kankantri. Gnarled black hands clutch the heavy axes. Forest giants are felled and parcels of land cleared, soon to be planted, thanks to government subsidies, with the whites' new coffee varieties. But sometimes the loggers suffer severe injuries. Who nurses them then? There are large wounds in their feet, deep enough for your fist to fit inside, filled with keloid scars – black feet, swollen and formless. The unbearable pain can be felt throughout the body. The stench from such wounds is too much for the others in the tent to bear. Amid the delightful fauna and flora of the primeval forest, a worker dies.

Employers promise whatever it takes to lure contract coolies to Suriname. The men were guaranteed eighty cents a day and the women sixty, even for days when circumstances beyond their control prevented them from working. Then came the depression. The highest officials were spared, and civil servants who earned up to f 12,000 a year had their salaries lowered by only five to ten percent. But the coolies – who are now put to work only two to three days a week, without any compensation for the days without work – have lost sixty to seventy-five percent of their wages. The men have gone from eighty to sixty cents a day, the women from sixty to forty. Weekly wages have dropped from f 4.80 to f 1.80.[7] The clever planters opened their own shops, usually leased to Chinese shopkeepers. The workers had no choice but to use the company store, and this injustice was all the easier to perpetrate because the Surinamese do not usually buy by the pound or kilogram but ask for ten cents' worth of this and twenty-five cents' worth of that. A worker who falls into debt this way has no hope of ever getting out of it. Seeds, or whatever else he needs to work the little plot of land that feeds his family, must be bought on credit from the planter. That means more debt to the plantation owner and empty bellies while waiting to harvest that patch of earth.

But if he tries to protest or flee, he will be brought back and punished.

And yet those workers, even if they just get two days of work a week, are enviable.

Meanwhile, it took the bloodbath of Red October before the government was willing to take any kind of serious look at the question of unemployment. Since then, it has sent the most troublesome and dangerous elements to the primeval forest, where, despite being untrained city people, they are made to tap wild rubber for which no market can be found or hunt for gold in completely worked-out mines. Almost all who took the risk of going there have returned with their health and spirits shattered. One of the people who bring their grievances to my table tells me you'd be better off hanging yourself – at least it would be a quick death.

My notebooks bulged with the stories of their suffering. And the witch hunt in the blanda press, in *De West* and *De Surinamer*, intensified.

The charge was led by the Catholic press. The "echoes from the missions" wailed about "misleading the poor."[8] At the same time, they spoke of "Communist creoles and black hussies." Hair-raising tales of murder and arson were whispered. And day after day, the motor squads rattled up and down my street. Yet what could I do, at that time, but plant the principle of solidarity in the people's hearts, that first little seed which I hope will grow into the strong, well-funded organization that we require.

But even that was dangerous.

Friends warned me that after Red October many comrades had been held in prison for months before, in the absence of any evidence against them, they were finally released. It cost them their jobs and their reputations here. Many who were less resilient were driven, as it were, into the miserable horde of criminals, which was growing at a terrifying rate. The direction of government policy is as clear as mud, and anyone who opposes that direction is hidden away – in the insane asylum Wolfenbuttel, if necessary, like Hugo de Vliet after his arrest in October 1931 and then the eighteen-year-old White in 1932, simply because he had written "down with X" on a fence.

The government's bravery when faced with unarmed workers from the city gives way to anxiety at the slightest thought that they may be linked to the militant elements in the forests. Since the meeting of workers and unemployed people in October 1931 where their delegate Adjangamang said "Un' denki Boni dede, ma en kra de ete!" – "You think Boni is dead, but his spirit lives on" rather than "You think Boni is dead, but his descendants are alive," as the official report claimed – there have been steps to wed greed with caution by charging several guilders a year for a license to carry arms. The resentment this provoked has been exacerbated since then by a fifty-cent tax for every log of wood chopped. And, meanwhile, the Ndyukas have been misled time and again by businessmen who refuse to pay for what they call rejected logs, which of course the Negroes cannot take back upriver with them and which the company uses anyway after the Ndyukas leave.

Almost every day representatives of the Ndyukas of the Upper Commewijne came to me, and I received a number of offers to bring weapons to my property in secret, offers I rejected in the most forceful terms. What I was after was organization, not a bloodbath.

But the very thing I was striving with all my might to avoid was only too clearly what some elements were aiming for. These people, who even now see the black race as doomed by its very nature to a life of crime, seem to have told themselves, "One good scare and they'll soon stop making trouble." The insight that a popular movement is brought about not by agitators, but by the economic condition of the people, was still beyond their grasp.

A few times before then, the procurator general (acting governor) had stood outside the fence around our property, observing the goings-on. On the morning of January 31, 1933, when the yard had already filled with Javanese visitors, a police squad led by Inspector F.S. Essed showed up and ordered everyone off the property.[9] This was my first opportunity to witness the typical British Indian form of non-violent resistance. However hard the officers pulled and tugged at the bodies of the squatting Javanese, not one of them raised a finger to stop them, but neither did they budge even a centimeter from where they sat. After about an hour of this performance, Inspector Essed turned to me in despair, saying, "Once the whites get here, you'll be more obedient."

Aware that we would eventually have to give way to their use of force and, intent on doing whatever it took to avert a violent clash, I replied, "Not for the whites, but because you are a man of my own race, I will ask them to leave the property." And, wonder of wonders, scarcely had I uttered those words to the crowd when the whole mass of Javanese people stood up in silence and left the property in a perfectly orderly fashion, although the police could not resist trying to make them hurry up by shoving and tugging on them, without the least provocation.[10]

In the meantime, exactly what I had hoped to avoid was happening: Saramaccastraat was filling with two or three thousand people, without any leadership or any well-defined goal, marching in the direction of the government headquarters. Still hoping to make the authorities see reason, I decided to go there by car, taking a slight detour so that I would not arrive at the head of a kind of procession. Speeding across the church square, which had already been cordoned off, I headed for the government building. When I asked to speak to the governor at once, I was told he was indisposed. No audience for me. Just a few moments after I arrived at police headquarters, the procurator general arrived in the governor's place, beet-red with outrage, and before I had the chance to say even a word, ordered the officers, "Arrest that fellow!"

Once I was behind the bars of my cell, inside a special barbed wire fence that was put up around the prison in great haste, I could not be an eyewitness to the events that followed. I heard about them from my wife and from a number of comrades later thrown in prison with me, and I read about them in the newspapers.

On February 4, the day after my arrest, a large crowd went to the public prosecutor's office to demand my immediate release. When the police threatened to shoot, several workers leapt forward, and opened their coats, baring their chests. "Here!" they said, "Go ahead and shoot, then at least we'll be free of our suffering!"

This shocked Van Haaren, who was looking on, and he told the crowd to return on Tuesday morning at eight (in other words, on February 7). "Then I will release De Kom."[11] This promise was heard by a number of Surinamese people, such as Doorson and Kaffee, and reported in *De Banier*.

When the crowd marched into the square outside the government building on Tuesday morning, Van Haaren had police officers and soldiers with carbines waiting for them.¹² But nothing out of the ordinary took place. The multitude proceeded calmly down Heerenstraat, which was not closed off. The mood was so peaceful that the whole crowd sat down calmly in the grass in front of the Palace Hotel and remained there for some minutes. But when, for no reason at all, one of these comrades was arrested, it prompted all of them to march on to the government building, where they announced that they would not leave until I was set free. There was still no commotion or violence whatsoever. But when they calmly refused to leave, the two salvos were fired that left two of them dead and twenty-two others severely wounded.¹³

After the deaths, the police felt it necessary to attack the panicked, fleeing crowd with sabers. In *De Banier* a person who had been present at the bloodbath wrote:

> I was an eyewitness when Inspector Kleinhout told a man he wasn't walking fast enough and beat him with his saber, so hard the man couldn't go any farther. Then an officer beat the same man some more with his rubber baton. What was done to the people – especially the poor Javanese, who tend to be physically weak – was beyond mere beating or mistreatment. Even after they were so battered that they were lying on the ground, the police went on bludgeoning them with the butts of their rifles. But those people didn't seek medical help afterwards because they were afraid they would be punished.

To once again demonstrate the thoroughly peaceful nature of the demonstration, which was broken up violently to scare people into submission, we offer a final quotation from our adversary *De Surinamer*, which wrote on February 10, "It is clear that the people were unarmed, since no weapons were found on any of the twenty-two who were brought to the hospital. Only Cyriell, who died, was armed – with a breadknife." That same evening, the police officers were officially honored for their response and rewarded with a beery celebration.[14]

When I think of the murdered comrades, of the wounded and maimed, of their distress and misery, then it seems almost trivial by comparison to mention my personal suffering: the vermin-infested cell, the ordeal of interrogation after interrogation and threat after threat, the pressure put on my wife (who was already unwell because of the unfamiliar climate), the searches of my house, the financial losses I suffered, and my unemployment after I returned to the Netherlands. All this serves merely as another example of the lawlessness and injustice that prevails in Suriname.

As early as February 3, the bourgeois newspaper *De Surinamer* reported, "De Kom endured everything stoically, not protesting anything but resigning himself to it all." This same newspaper also commented, "So the arrest took place without any certainty of prosecution." These words were prophetic, as became clear when, on May 10, I was unexpectedly put on board the *Rensselaer* with my family. And even the newspaper *De West*, ultra-loyal to the government, could not help but observe, "How unfortunate that the justice authorities were not quicker to realize that formal evidence of guilt might be difficult to supply. Of course, it is impossible for an outsider to consider all the circumstances that caused delays, but in any case, it is unfortunate that it took three months before this decision could be made, and that this delay so prolonged the tensions in the colony."[15]

We fear that De Kom's departure will not bring the "tensions in the colony" to an end. "They've had a good scare now," blood has flowed, but the suffering continues. Jacob Kanna, Indian captain, went to the government secretary to request a little food for his thirty famished fellow villagers.[16] He was flatly rejected. The maroons, too, sometimes suffer famine. Unemployment is rising. Mr. A.G. Putscher, a member of the Colonial States of Suriname, criticized the governor's policy in the sharpest possible terms in a speech delivered on July 12, 1933 in The Hague in *Twee Steden*:[17]

> The poor mood in Suriname also has a deeper source: the general understanding that the administration's policy is completely inadequate and falls far short of what is called for by conditions in Suriname in this worrying time. The measures taken there merely allow these bad conditions to go on unchecked. Nothing is done to stop the deterioration; not a single germ of hope is planted for the flowering of new life and prosperity. This total lack of initiative, organizational capacity, and talent for government is the true source of the dissatisfaction brewing at every level of Surinamese society ... It is right to ask: If rice and maize cultivation had been improved and encouraged and banana cultivation resumed, in the spirit of Mr. Brandon and Mr. Fernandes,[18] would the results not have prevented the miserable conditions that spread under Mr. Rutgers's supervision until dissatisfaction led to disturbance of the peace and had to be suppressed through bloodshed and the taking of lives?

But Governor Rutgers hurriedly cut short his brief career in the colony and returned to the Netherlands, taking up a seat in the Lower House of Parliament, where he is generally acknowledged as an expert in discussions of the interests of Suriname.

Before his departure he took his final measures: "The administration will be prepared for the possibility that the events of October 1931 and February 1933 will repeat themselves, if perhaps in a different form."

In other words, the administration knows that growing misery can lead to growing resistance, and it plans to thwart any form of organization among the Surinamese, much as it brought about the dissolution of the SAWO in 1932 for supposed activity "in the religious and political domains."[19]

But the opinion leaders in the press applaud.

The July 6, 1933, issue of the *Handelsblad* has the gall to remark, "One of Governor Rutgers's greatest accomplishments, without a doubt, is that he managed to reduce the amount of public support in the budget, despite major expenditures for crisis support and a large decrease in revenue."[20]

When a Surinamese person dies, it means little to the *Handelsblad*, as long as he has the good will to die on the cheap.

But as events have shown, the good will of Suriname's people is beginning to dry up.

Sranan, my fatherland.

One day I hope to see you again.

The day all your misery has been wiped away.

Glossary of Surinamese Terms

Most of the distinctively Surinamese terms used come from Sranantongo, the language of Suriname's Afro-Surinamese community. The spelling of Sranantongo terms has been modernized to reflect present-day norms, clarify the pronunciation, facilitate the use of contemporary Sranantongo dictionaries, and make the book more accessible to today's Surinamese readers. A few terms from Surinamese Dutch and other languages are also explained here.

This glossary is limited to single words and some two-word phrases. Translations of entire sentences or passages in Sranantongo are generally given in the main body of the book or in the notes. Where De Kom offers a Dutch gloss for a Sranantongo word in the main body of the original book, I give a corresponding English gloss in the translation.

aboma sneki	anaconda
angalampu	the flowering shrub *Hibiscus schizopetalus*, literally "hanging lamp"
Anitri lerimans	Moravian preachers
bakra	white (often derogatory)
barklaki	woody plant in the genus *Eschweilera*
baskita	basket

blanda	Dutch or white (often pejorative, originally from the Dutch East Indies, derived from "Holland")
blauwdas	the prized songbird *Euphonia finschi*, a type of finch
blawforki	blue-gray tanager
fayalobi	the flowering plant *Ixora coccinea*, literally "fiery love"
fayaworon	firefly
gadofowru	house wren
grikibi	great kiskadee
kabugru	definitions vary: a person either of mixed Amerindian and African descent, or of three-quarters Afro-Surinamese and one-quarter white descent
kankantri	kapok tree, *Cieba pentandra*, sometimes an object of worship
kantra	piece of bran or husk
klarun	amaranth
koki	cook
koto	traditional Surinamese dress worn on festive occasions
kotomisi	woman wearing a koto (see above)
krabasi	calabash, gourd
manya	mango
owru kuku	owl
p'pokaitongo	the colorful perennial herb *Heliconia psittacorum*, literally "parrot tongues"
pakira	collared peccary
patata	denigrating term for a white person, literally "potato"
pyaw	form of gambling of Chinese origin, popular among the Chinese and creole communities in early twentieth-century Suriname
raison	Surinamese stringed musical instrument

sinsin   *Mimosa pudica* plant; the leaves droop
                  or close in response to touch
Srananliba   Suriname River
tigriman   a domesticated male songbird, often
                  a twa twa (a great-billed seedfinch),
                  aged 12 to 24 months. Age categories
                  for songbirds are used in birdsong
                  competitions, a traditional Surinamese
                  pastime
truli   *Manicaria saccifera* palm tree (or its
                  leaves)
wiswisi   black-bellied or white-faced whistling
                  duck
yamsi   purple yam

Notes

"Sranan," Our Fatherland

1 TN: De Kom uses the Dutch-language Surinamese names of the yellow lapacho ("groenhart," literally "greenheart") and the wacapou ("bruinhart," literally "brownheart"); these have been translated literally to draw attention to the color words and the recurrence of "heart."

2 TN: In Dutch, the two terms "het Westen" and "de West," both of which can be translated as "the West," have contrasting meanings. Here, De Kom uses "het Westen" to refer to "the West" in a traditional European cultural sense, meaning Europe and perhaps also North America. The western colonies of the Netherlands, in the Caribbean region, were referred to as "de West."

The Era of Slavery

1 TN: Albert Helman is the pen name of Lodewijk Lichtveld (1903–1996), a member of Suriname's "colored" elite and one of the most prolific and influential Surinamese writers of the twentieth century. He first came to the attention of Dutch-language readers in the 1920s, when he published the volume of poetry *De glorende dag* ("The Dawning

Day") and *Zuid Zuid-West* ("South Southwest"), a novel critical of the colonial regime in Suriname. He was a major literary inspiration for De Kom, who quotes from his work and refers to him many times in *We Slaves of Suriname*. The quotation here is from *Zuid Zuid-West*, which is available online in Dutch at https://www.dbnl.org/tekst/ helm003zuid02_01/index.php.

2 Jan Jacob Hartsinck, *Beschryving van Guiana of de wilde kust in Zuid-America*, Amsterdam, Gerrit Tielenburg, 1770. One of the oldest and best-known works about Suriname, quoting from the most significant letters, advisory reports, ordinances, conventions, and charters. Hartsinck, whose father had served as director of the Society of Suriname for twenty-five years, was assisted in compiling this book by the colonial secretary, Van Meel, and other distinguished residents of Suriname, and had access to the archives, resolutions, acts, and ordinances of the colonial adminis- tration. This ensured the complete reliability of his work. [Dutch edition available online: https://www.dbnl.org/tekst/ hart038besc01_01/]

3 J. Wolbers, *Geschiedenis van Suriname*, Amsterdam, S. Emmeringh, 1861, p. 17.

In our book, we will often refer to this excellent reference work about Suriname, which stands out all the more for its objectivity and sense of truth and justice when you consider that it was written in an era when slavery had not yet been abolished in Suriname.

The following passages from the preface to the work of this authentically devout and liberal writer, who made a powerful case for the abolition of slavery, attest to the credibility of the facts reported by Wolbers:

> An especially rich source was opened up to me at the National Archives ['s Rijks-Archief]. There, in the minutes of Governors and Councilors, Governors' diaries, and other official documents, I found the most important particulars ... Although it was a tiring task to go through those many thick folio manuscripts, the effort was richly rewarded by the discovery of particulars that shed a bright light on matters which had previously remained shrouded in darkness. (p. II)

No one will ever have any grounds for accusing me of having written untruths or twisted the facts or presented them in a false light. (p. IV)

[Dutch edition available online: https://www.dbnl.org/tekst/wolb002gesc01_01/index.php]

4 Werner Sombart, *Der Bourgeois*, Leipzig, Duncker & Humblot, 1913, pp. 96–98. [Quotation from the English translation *The Quintessence of Capitalism* by Mortimer Epstein, New York, E.P. Dutton, 1915, pp. 69–71. See https://babel.hathitrust.org/cgi/pt?id=inu.39000002373301&view=1up&seq=7]

5 TN: I quote from the published English translation of *Der Bourgeois*; see also the endnote. De Kom's Dutch translation from the original German mentions that Columbus also brought back "the legend of the gilded prince"; this phrase is missing from the English edition that I consulted. There are other slight differences of nuance and emphasis between De Kom's Dutch translation and the published English version. Note also that "undertaker" is used in this passage in the sense of "entrepreneur."

6 Wolbers, pp. 26–27.

7 Bartolomé de las Casas was a Spanish priest who spent many years in the Americas. Filled with pity for the miserable lives of the indigenous people, who were worked to exhaustion in a monstrous manner by their new masters, especially in the gold mines, he proposed the importation of Negro slaves. His work *Brevísima relación de la destrucción de las Indias* (1552) was translated into almost all European languages. [Translated into English as *A Brief Account of the Destruction of the Indies*, London, R. Hewson, 1689]

8 Hartsinck, vol. II, p. 585.

9 TN: The States General was the supreme authority of the Dutch Republic and evolved into the present Dutch parliament, which is still known by that name.

10 Wolbers, p. 837. The entire charter is reprinted word for word in Wolbers, pp. 834–846.

11 Art. XVIII, Wolbers, p. 844.

12 TN: De Kom alludes to two tales of high-seas adventure then popular among Dutch readers: Heinrich Hauser's non-fiction account *A Swan-Song of Sailing Ships* (the Dutch title and the original German title translate literally as "The Last Sailing Ship") and Arthur van Schendel's novel *Het fregatschip Johanna Maria* ("The Frigate *Johanna Maria*").

13 Diary of Governor J.J. Mauricius, Wolbers, p. 121.

14 See also W. Bosman, *Nauwkeurige beschrijving van de Guinese Goud-, tand- en slavekust*, Amsterdam, Isaak Stokmans, 1709, pp, 149–151. "This act [of branding] appears, if I am not mistaken, rather cruel, half barbaric, to Your Excellency; yet, as it takes place out of necessity, it must therefore go on in the same manner."

15 Letter from Pinson Bonham to Earl Bathurst, February 9, 1814, Wolbers, p. 567. (During the period of British rule in Suriname, Bonham was governor from 1811 to 1816.)

16 Letter from Pinson Bonham to Earl Bathurst, July 14, 1831; Wolbers, p. 567.

17 Genesis 9:25. See also verse 27: "God shall enlarge Japheth, and he shall dwell in the tents of Shem; and Canaan shall be his servant."

18 Johan Picardt, *Korte beschryvinge van eenige vergetene en verborgene antiquiteiten*, Amsterdam, Gerrit van Goedesbergh, 1660, p. 9.

19 Minutes of the Governor and Councilors [Notulen van Gouverneur en Raden], December 24, 1745, in Wolbers, pp. 131–132.

20 Wolbers, pp. 288–289.

21 Minutes of the Governor and Councilors, August 4, 1761, in Wolbers, p. 290.

22 For example, see Hartsinck, vol. II, p. 646: "Van Sommelsdijck decreed that from then on no one would be permitted any longer to maim his slaves or punish them with death – which left quite a bit of latitude."

23 Minutes of the Governor and Councilors, August 30 and September 18, 1799, in Wolbers, p. 494.

24 Wolbers, pp. 494–495.

25 Journal of Governor Jan Jacob Mauricius, September 6,

1750. His further remarks are also noteworthy: "These documents show yet again that accidents on plantations are generally the result of mismanagement." Wolbers, p. 132.

26 Minutes of the Governor and Councilors, December 1, 1800, in Wolbers, p. 494.

27 Mauricius in *Recueil van egte stukken en bewyzen, door Salomon du Plessis*, 1752, vol. II, section 107, p. 517.

28 *Recueil van egte stukken*, vol. II, section 16, p. 185.

29 John Gabriel Stedman, *Narrative of a Five Years Expedition against the Revolted Negroes of Surinam*, 1790 (manuscript) and 1796 (first published edition). "[T]he prisoners are generally present ... and instantly tied up ... when the flogging begins, with men, women, or children, without exception. ... during which they alternately repeat, "Dankee, massera," (Thank you, master). In the mean time he [the planter] stalks up and down with his overseer, affecting not so much as to hear their cries." [Quotation from the edition in Eighteenth Century Collections Online; see https://quod. lib.umich.edu/e/ecco/004897533.0001.002/1:3.3?rgn=div 2;view=fulltext. This edition more closely resembles the Dutch edition quoted by De Kom here than does the critical edition edited by Richard and Sally Price and published in 1988, listed in the bibliography on p. 26.]

Stedman, Scottish by birth, was a volunteer with the rank of captain under Fourgeaud in the expedition against the maroons from 1772 to 1777.

Besides the unabridged Dutch translation, there was also a French translation, as well as abridged German and Dutch translations. Stedman's frequent sharp criticism of circumstances in Suriname was greatly resented by the Dutch. The words of the God-fearing writer M.D. Teenstra in his book *De negerslaven van Suriname* ["The Negro Slaves of Suriname"] are worth noting here: "but if this British captain has exaggerated many things, yet there is also a great deal that is true; truths that those in Suriname do not wish to hear are called ungrateful libel there, because when a person has been welcomed as a guest, he should not make public how the slaves there are treated; that is the crux of it," pp. 322–323.

30 Hartsinck, vol. II, pp. 741ff.
31 Wolbers, p. 182.
32 Stedman, *Narrative of a Five Years Expedition*, p. 49 in the Price & Price edition.
33 Wolbers, p. 187.
34 The "suspended" state involved tying the slave's hands together with a strong rope and then dangling him from the branch of a tree or a beam of the house, some distance above the ground. A fifty-pound weight was hung from his feet to prevent him from kicking or swinging back and forth, after which he was flogged with a tough braid of cane with sharp thorns. [TN: originally a footnote]
35 Wolbers, p. 292. Crommelin proposed a number of articles intended to keep the mistreatment of slaves in check; one was that those "guilty of taking the life of any slave will receive corporal or capital punishment." The Noble Councilors would not endorse this provision. While they did acknowledge that there were some plantation owners "who were so evil-natured that they did not hesitate to destroy their own capital," they insisted that these degenerates were the exceptions. They also expressed the opinion "that it is of the utmost importance that the slaves not be led to question the belief that their masters have legal authority over life and death, and that they would be uncontrollable if they realized that their masters could receive corporal or capital punishment for beating a slave to death." Wolbers, pp. 293–294.
36 According to the Charter [Octrooi] of 1682, criminal justice was the responsibility of the Governing Council [Hof van Politie en Criminele Justitie]. The chairman of this body was the governor; the other members included the Commander, in the role of First Councilor, and nine unpaid Councilors selected from among the most distinguished residents. There was also an advisory member, the Councilor-Prosecutor, the only one belonging to the legal profession, who was also the deputy head of the public prosecution department. [TN: This body, consisting of the governor and a number of prominent planters serving as councilors, is referred to by various names in Dutch,

both in the primary sources and by De Kom in this book. It was both an executive and a judicial body. I follow the example of the historian Karwan Fatah-Black in referring to it consistently in English as the Governing Council; see e.g. his article "The usurpation of legal roles by Suriname's Governing Council, 1669–1816."]

37 Minutes of the Governor and Councilors, May 1, 1729, Wolbers, pp. 133–134.

38 Minutes of the Governor and Councilors, August 2, 1737, Wolbers, pp. 133–134.

39 Minutes of the Governor and Councilors, April 29, 1732, Wolbers, pp. 133–134.

40 Minutes of the Governor and Councilors, December 14, 1730, Wolbers, pp. 145–146.

41 Minutes of the Governor and Councilors, December 16 and 18, 1762, Wolbers, pp. 290–291.

42 Minutes of the Governor and Councilors, February 27 and September 12, 1747, Wolbers, pp. 287–288.

43 Minutes of the Governor and Councilors, May 2, 1731, Wolbers, pp. 130–131.

44 TN: Here De Kom quotes a version of a then well-known line by P.C. Hooft, a canonical poet of the Dutch Golden Age: "Mijn hand is hard doch liefelijk mijn gemoed."

45 Wolbers, p. 135.

46 TN: Roughly equivalent to €180,000 in 2021 according to the International Institute of Social History conversion tool at https://iisg.amsterdam/nl/onderzoek/projecten/hpw/calculate.php.

47 TN: The Brothers of Tilburg are a Catholic religious order founded in the Dutch city of Tilburg and active in various countries. The historical figures mentioned are Dutch naval officers, then (and even now) celebrated as heroes.

48 TN: Claudius Civilis was the leader of the Batavian rebellion against the Romans, known to present-day historians as Gaius Julius Civilis and long mythologized in the Netherlands as the father of the Dutch people. The Act of Abjuration was the declaration of independence from Spain by many provinces of the Netherlands. William the Silent, or William of Orange, was the foremost leader of the Dutch

Revolt against Spanish rule and the ancestor of the present Royal Family.

49 TN: Boni, Baron, and Joli Coeur are discussed at length below.

50 TN: Joannes Benedictus van Heutsz was a Dutch military leader, known for his role in the Aceh War, and the later governor-general of the Dutch East Indies.

51 TN: "Child of State" was the title of William II's only child, the future William III of England.

52 TN: An Amsterdam pound was 494 grams.

53 TN: This settlement, later abandoned when the Jewish community moved to Paramaribo, is now best known under the name of Jodensavanne, a variant of the name given by De Kom ("djoe Savanna" in the original Dutch).

54 TN: A Surinamese acre, or akker, is 4,294 square meters.

55 TN: Probably Casper (or Caspar) Robijn.

56 Surinamese stringed musical instrument. [TN: originally a footnote]

57 TN: The Rasphuis was a prison in Amsterdam.

58 Surinamese Book of Acts [placaatboek], July 7, 1685, July 10, 1687, November 8, 1698, February 20, 1717, and May 18, 1718, and Minutes of the Governor and Councilors, December 7, 1742. Wolbers, pp. 138–139.

59 Hartsinck, vol. II, p. 757, gives a total of about five to six thousand.

60 Hartsinck, vol. II, pp. 700–722, gives a detailed description of this invasion. He is also the source of other interesting figures such as the following: 734 Negro slaves were exported for the price of *f* 350 per person and a number of Indians for the total price of *f* 2,300.

61 Hartsinck, vol. II, p. 740.

62 TN: In Greek mythology, the Danaids were condemned to spend eternity filling a bathtub with a hole in the bottom.

63 Wolbers, pp. 140–141. [Wolbers italicizes only the phrase "notwithstanding all the torments with fire and blows"; the italics in this passage were otherwise added by De Kom.]

64 TN: In 1932, at the initiative of justice minister Jan Donner, blasphemy had been made punishable by law in

the Netherlands, in response to a number of controversial publications by freethinkers and communists.

65 Hartsinck, vol. II, pp. 768–771.
66 Wolbers, p. 149; also mentioned in Stedman.
67 On these peace treaties, see Hartsinck, vol. II, pp. 755–813, and Stedman, vol. I, pp. 78–96.
68 Stedman, vol. I, p. 90. See also Wolbers, p. 155.
69 TN: A reference to George Duhamel's *Scènes de la vie future*, an account of the French author's travels in the United States in late 1929, which expresses horror at American consumerism, greed, and industrial capitalism. The English translation is entitled *America the Menace: Scenes from the Life of the Future*.
70 TN: De Kom's use of "volks-," translated here as "folk," could also be rendered as "popular" or "people's" and has anti-capitalist political resonances.
71 See also Wolbers, pp. 159–160.
72 Minutes of the Governor and Councilors, September 25, 1772, Wolbers, pp. 331–332,
73 Minutes of the Governor and Councilors, June 30, 1772, Wolbers, p. 338.
74 Stedman, vol. I, p. 303.
75 A detailed eyewitness account of this expedition can be found in Stedman, vol. III, pp. 1–53.
76 Wolbers, p. 352.
77 Wolbers, pp. 352–353.
78 TN: Jacob Cats was a poet of the Dutch Golden Age known for his light verse and moralistic poems.
79 P.F. Roos, in the poem "Suriname verheerlijkt" ["In Praise of Suriname"], p. 297 of the collection *Surinaamse Mengelpoëzy*, Amsterdam, 1804. Roos was the chairman of the Surinaamse Lettervrienden [Friends of Surinamese Literature]. Allow us to quote a few more lines from the poem:

> Instruct your children in their honest civic duties;
> Teach them to raise up temples in praise of liberty!
> [...]
> Rejoice, O citizens! Women and men alike!

Rejoice, O husbands, and rejoice, beloved wives
and scions, at the good awaiting Suriname!
The planters' hope is dawning; and agriculture smiles;
Trade, which had languished, now once more begins to
thrive;
Shipping is picking up; the peoples come and go.
It seems prosperity has found a new abode.
Africa's coast, rebuilt, as in an earlier age,
Will serve us as a warehouse packed with sturdy slaves!

80 TN: Batenburg's title and initials, omitted in the original, can be found in vol. 12 of *The Naval Chronicle*, July–December 1804, pp. 83–85.

81 Wolbers, p. 455.

82 Letter from G. Gramstown to Archer, February 23, 1806. Wolbers, p. 555.

83 TN: Before the revolutionary regime in the Netherlands, the annual holiday of Prinsjesdag had been an occasion to celebrate and display loyalty to the governing House of Orange.

84 TN: Johannes van den Bosch was never governor but did preside over the administration briefly as commissioner-general; see e.g. https://en.wikipedia.org/wiki/List_of_colonial_governors_of_Suriname or the Dutch-language *Encyclopedie van Suriname*.

85 M.D. Teenstra, *De Negerslaven in de kolonie Suriname*, Dordrecht, 1842, pp. 267–268 and 287–292. The entire trial and the judgment, which Teenstra calls "a match for the horrors of the barbaric Middle Ages," are described by him at length.

86 TN: De Kom situates the events of his narrative relative to historical developments that would have been familiar to his Dutch readers. Jan van Speijk was a Dutch naval officer in the Belgian Revolution revered as a hero by the Dutch for choosing to blow up his own ship rather than surrender it. Jacobus Bellamy was a late eighteenth-century Dutch poet from a working-class background, a supporter of French Revolutionary ideals and opponent of sentimental poetry, who aimed to bring poetry closer to the language of everyday life.

87 TN: John Bent submitted a complaint about illegal smuggling of slaves, which Van Heeckeren rejected. Halberstadt was a colonial official in Suriname who became a whistle-blower after being discharged from his duties by Van Heeckeren on unproven charges of misconduct.

88 A. Halberstadt, *Kolonisatie van Europeanen te Suriname*. After many years of searching for a publisher for this book, the author ultimately published it at his own expense. The book constitutes a bitter and very fierce indictment of the colonial regime. Two other works by the same author are *Een standbeeld voor de Graaf van den Bosch* and *Vrijmaking der slaven in Suriname*.

89 TN: De Kom appears to imply that Van Raders was dishonorably discharged from his post. Other sources contradict this; see e.g. the Dutch-language Wikipedia entry https://nl.wikipedia.org/wiki/Reinier_Frederik_van_Raders, based on the *Encyclopaedie van Nederlandsch West-Indië* (1914–1917).

90 Wolbers, p. 691.

91 Petition from interested parties in Amsterdam to the Minister of the Colonies [Adres van belanghebbenden te Amsterdam aan de minister van Koloniën], October 31, 1843. Wolbers, p. 693.

92 Wolbers, pp. 693–694.

93 Wolbers's remarks on this petition include the following: "This document is a tissue of lies. Ignorance was pretended of matters known to all. Suspicions were cooked up that no one entertained. The facts were twisted, distorted ..." (p. 696).

94 Wolbers, p. 699.

95 TN: In contemporary Dutch, "spekkoeken" are sweet layer cakes; it is unclear whether De Kom is referring to something similar here. The term may also mean something like "cakes of lard," "pancakes fried in lard," or "pancakes with bacon."

96 Wolbers, pp. 707–708.

97 TN: Surinamese slaves had not traditionally been allowed to wear shoes.

98 Wolbers, pp. 714–717. See also the Report of the State

Commission for the Proposal of Measures regarding the Slaves in the Dutch Colonies [Rapport der Staatscommissie tot het voorstellen van maatregelen t.a.v. de slaven in de Nederlandse koloniën], 1855.

99 Report of the Commission of the Lower House of Parliament [Verslag der Commissie uit de Tweede Kamer], session of May 8, 1861. Wolbers, p. 754.

100 In this circular letter, Tank wrote, "I would find my own conduct reprehensible, Gentlemen!, if I did not frankly and honestly tell you what I believe, as befits a free Dutchman. That is why I do not wish to keep it from you ... that I have not seen slaves so mistreated anywhere else as they are in Suriname. Where else than among us is a Negro punished merely for submitting a complaint; where else is he so brutally punished as among us?"

Wolbers comments, "If Tank's manly language impressed readers in the Netherlands, those in Suriname were infuriated" (p. 719).

101 Wolbers, p. 720.

102 Maria Louise Elisabeth Vlier, *Geschiedenis van Suriname*, p. 213.

103 From the fifth volume of *Théorie des Loix Civiles*, by S.H.N. Linguet (1736–1794), as quoted by H.P.G. Quack in *De socialisten*, vol. I, pp. 346–347. This work, which is mainly a criticism of Montesquieu's *Esprit des Lois*, drew the attention of thinkers including Karl Marx, who remarked in *Das Kapital*, "Linguet cast aside Montesquieu's illusory 'Spirit of Law' with the single statement, 'The spirit of law is property.'"

104 In America, the constitutional amendments of 1865 abolished slavery and involuntary servitude. The plantations of the planters in the South were abandoned en masse, which led to a severe shortage of workers. So the planters capitulated and entered into employment contracts with their liberated slaves that specified wages of ten to fifteen dollars a month, giving the former slaves at least enough to live on. How much better these conditions were than the ones confronting the Surinamese after the abolition of slavery.

105 Wolbers, pp. 776–777.
106 Wolbers, p. 775.

The Era of "Freedom"

1 See also the report on the work of Freule J.W. van Lynden for the Moravian Church in Paramaribo, published in *Ons Suriname*, a Moravian mission periodical, in July 1933. We quote:

> The undersigned was deeply affected by the poverty suffered throughout the city, and especially by how little the Church, as such, did or could do to alleviate this struggle ...
>
> Will you follow me on my daily trips through "dark Paramaribo"? Never fear, I will not take you to slums and alleys where the courage of a Salvation Army soldier is required. Dark Paramaribo can be found in the sunny streets of our city. Behind the front houses where those blessed with more earthly goods dwell are the "properties" with the many, many homes of the poor, the former slave dwellings.
>
> Our mode of transportation is the bicycle. Walking is too tiring. But keep in mind that our streets are not asphalted. Strong lungs and strong seat springs are required. Some streets look much like the lanes through the heath in Gelderland and Brabant. In the dry season, large distances must be covered on foot after all, because sand and dust make cycling impossible. When the rain comes, this situation improves rapidly. But soon enough, you no longer know what to prefer. Sometimes the mud rises above your pedals ...
>
> ... The average number of home visits was 100 per month. Whenever possible, I spent five afternoons a week on home visits. These visits meant a few days without the worst hunger. Hundreds of households suffer real famine; the children aged one to three often have liver disease, which makes them thin, underweight, and too short, sad little things to behold, as a result of malnutrition or, since most mothers breastfeed their children until the age of one year or older, of malnutrition of the mother..

Friends, it was seventy years ago this year that the Negro slaves of Suriname were declared free. It was *only* seventy years ago that the Netherlands came to the realization that the money earned in Suriname was stained with blood. Are we not at fault? None of us should say that we had no shares in Surinamese plantations and are therefore not to blame. Our guilt is collective! Shouldn't we all work together to pay back a little of this debt, the consequences of which are now coming to light in such a shocking way? ...

But we Dutch people, Dutch Christians, what are we doing?

2 TN: *De Banier*, quoted several times by De Kom in the course of the book, was a Surinamese newspaper known for being critical of the colonial administration and voicing the concerns of ordinary Surinamese people.

3 TN: Dry grounds are vegetable gardens protected from flooding by small dikes. A dabree is a shallow tray in which balata latex is coagulated. "Cutting lines" sometimes relates to clearing strips of forest but may in this case refer to making cuts in the bark of balata trees to release the rubber.

4 TN: De Kom is contrasting the Supreme Labor Council (Hoge Raad van Arbeid), a prewar Dutch institution for social dialogue between organized labor, industry, and government authorities, with the Marxist concept of the workers' council (Dutch: arbeidersraad), a central idea of communism, which was especially influential in Dutch communist thought in the early twentieth century.

5 TN: The Dutch word "rijk" can mean either "empire" or "kingdom" (for which the more precise term "koninkrijk" also exists) and is often used where "state" or "nation" might be used in English. So where De Kom refers to the Dutch kingdom, state, or nation, he is often reminding the reader of that state's imperialist nature.

6 TN: "The Dutch legislature": in other words, the Dutch parliament in the Netherlands, known as the States General, as opposed to any Surinamese institution. De Kom's description of these two members of parliament as "Suriname specialists" can safely be interpreted as

ironic. G.H. Kersten was the first representative of a conservative Calvinist party, the SGP, in the lower house of the Dutch parliament, and A. Braat, known as "Farmer Braat," was the leader of a Dutch farmers' party, the Plattelandersbond, which was opposed to modern urban society.

7 TN: The Vaderlandsche Club (Fatherland Club) in the Dutch East Indies was formed in 1929 in opposition to Indonesian nationalist movements and sought to strengthen Dutch authority in that colony.

8 TN: The "people from Indonesia" to whom De Kom refers here were not Javanese or other people indigenous to the Indonesian archipelago but white people with experience in the colonial administration in the Dutch East Indies.

9 TN: After the Dutch aristocracy was officially abolished in 1848, the titles "jonkheer" and "jonkvrouw" remained in use for the members of formerly aristocratic families.

10 TN: By using the term "Indonesian," De Kom expresses his solidarity with the independence movement in the Dutch East Indies.

11 See also Dr. Lampe, *Suriname, Sociaal-hygiënische Beschouwing*, p. 5: "The growth of the Javanese population in Suriname tends to be so feeble that left to their own devices – in other words, without further immigration – this race will die out in Suriname, and will do so in the fairly near future."

12 TN: An allusion to the tragic love story of Saijah and Adinda in Multatuli's great nineteenth-century Dutch novel *Max Havelaar*, well known to many of De Kom's readers, which protests the misdeeds of the Dutch colonial authorities in Indonesia.

13 TN: In Suriname, "creole" is a term, now somewhat outdated, for the descendants of people freed from slavery. It is close in meaning to the contemporary term "Afro-Surinamer," but the latter is often taken also to include Suriname's maroons, the descendants of people who *escaped* from slavery.

14 TN: The annual income from a full-time working-class job in the Netherlands in the early 1930s, when De Kom

was writing, was around 1,500 to 1,700 guilders a year (although unemployment was rife).

15 In the contract recently concluded with the All Line regarding a high-speed connection to Curaçao, the colonial administration included an explicit provision that the rates charged by this company, which completes the voyage in four days, may not exceed those of the Koninklijke Nederlandse Stoomboot-Maatschappij (Royal Netherlands Steamship Company), which takes ten days.

16 TN: The German sentence means "A man's trade will nourish him" and can be found in slightly different forms (normally with "Handwerk" rather than "Ambacht") in various sources, including the work of Werner Sombart, an author quoted elsewhere in *We Slaves of Suriname*. The quotation that follows is described as being from *De economische en financiële toestand der kolonie Suriname*, p. 64. This presumably refers to the 1911 report of a Dutch government commission, also known as the Rapport Bos ("Bos Report").

17 TN: This appears to be another quotation from the Rapport Bos from 1911, mentioned in the previous note, with italics perhaps added by De Kom.

18 TN: The United Fruit Company is the American corporation now known as Chiquita Brands International.

19 Governor Lely's explanatory memorandum on the banana plans stated that *f* 750,000 was the maximum the state would budget for this banana experiment.

Appendix VI to the aforementioned paper by the financial administrator, dated October 28, 1910, shows the actual spending:

1906 expenditure		*f* 144,328.33½
1907 expenditure		*f* 503,434.10
Negative balance as of Dec. 31, 1908		*f* 647,762.43½
1908 expenditure	*f* 569,717.86	
1908 revenue	*f* 96,474.62½	
Expenditure in excess of revenue	*f* 473,243.23½	
		f 473,243.23½
Negative balance as of Dec. 31, 1908		*f* 1,121,005.67

1909 expenditure	ƒ 651,085.21½	
1909 revenue	ƒ 275,094.23	
Expenditure in excess of revenue	ƒ 375,990.98½	
		ƒ 375,990.98½
Negative balance as of Dec. 31, 1909		ƒ 1,496,996.65½
1910 expenditure (first six months)	ƒ 318,059.30	
1910 revenue	ƒ 134,696.25½	
Expenditure in excess of revenue	ƒ 183,363.04½	
		ƒ 183,363.04½
Negative balance as of June 30, 1910		ƒ 1,680,359.70

20 TN: De Kom does not indicate the source of this quotation.

21 Two hundred guilders per hectare for cultivating banana fields that had been written off; three hundred guilders per hectare for cultivating new fields. [TN: originally a footnote]

22 In the January 1934 issue of the *West-Indische Gids*, A.J. Simons wrote in his article "Het verval van Suriname" (pp. 299–308): "The legend of the 'lazy Negro' was fabricated in the days of slavery; it has now been modified into the people's unwillingness to work in farming. That amounts to looking for the cause of the country's decline in the last place it is to be found …".

Mr. Simons then gives ten reasons for this decline, five of which we list here:

I. The complete lack of expertise about Suriname in the Netherlands and above all in the Dutch government.

When Minister Colijn says that "even if he did have the millions, he would not know what to do with Suriname," he is not announcing anything new, but remaining loyal to tradition and persisting in a misguided government policy, the result of a lack of knowledge of this country, because of which we are sinking ever deeper into the mud.

II. The assignment of officials from the Dutch East Indies to Suriname.

In the words of a famous Dutch statesman, "It would be better to put any old village mayor in charge of the West Indian colonies; he would as a rule be more suitable than the most qualified East Indian officials."

III. Our bloated public administration.

Suriname is a colony of officials, you sometimes hear, and this is perfectly true. Does it tell us nothing that every year more than 3 million, or seventy-plus percent of the projected budget revenues, goes to the bureaucracy, and this when the population is 150,000? As long as we are governed by East Indian officials, who are used to living in the lap of luxury and surrounding themselves with an army of subordinates like Eastern potentates, the shears of austerity will never be wielded and Suriname will sink deeper and deeper..

VIII. The high taxes, which are raised even higher when times are hard.

IX. The outdated method of agriculture.

The author ends his article with the words, "I hope that I have now explained Suriname's decline and refuted the pretense that its decline is the fault of its people."

23 TN: The first line is a Surinamese proverb in Sranantongo; the second line gives a translation.

24 TN: "Troelstra's song" refers to *Morgenrood* ("Red Sunrise"), a socialist song well known in the Dutch-speaking world, composed by Otto Willem de Nobel with lyrics by Dirk Jelles Troelstra. The Wilhelmus is the Dutch national anthem.

25 TN: A Latin proverb: "Deliberat Roma, perit Saguntum." The Carthaginian general Hannibal won a crucial military victory in Saguntum (near modern-day Sagunto, Spain) because the Romans failed to act in time, even though they received advance warning of his plans.

Reunion and Farewell

1 *De Surinamer*, no. I (1933), states, "Few people had any idea that De Kom was coming, but he was announced to be a communist, and that aroused widespread interest. The interest in De Kom as an individual was growing when, upon his arrival, the police decided they should make an exceptionally great show of authority ...

"Wherever that man went, he was followed in the most intrusive manner, by three former police officers who had been dismissed from duty: Baal, Leeuwin, and Kolf, in alternation. They had been hired for this specific job...

"This response was generally decried."

2 TN: Hoffman's drops were a tranquilizer; in other words, the whites must have been very nervous.

3 This label was incorrect; I was not and am not a member of the Communist Party.

4 Even the Suriname correspondent to the *Algemeen Handelsblad* concluded (on February 7, 1933), "For years, the administration has acted as if all is for the best in this best of all possible worlds. Has the administration ever shown in word or gesture that it has any concern for the future? Something is brewing in Suriname and has been brewing for some time. But the administration never gives a moment's thought to that. It blames every conflict on the other side."

And Mr. Putscher, a member of the Colonial States, said in his speech in The Hague on July 12, 1993 (p. 6 of the report), "If the administration had understood that governing is a matter of constructive initiative and foresight, then Suriname could, beyond any shadow of a doubt, have been prevented from descending into unemployment, discontent, disorderliness, and bloodshed ..."

5 *De Surinamer*, no. 10, 1933, "No one knew what De Kom planned to speak about, but he is a communist, and that is more than enough reason to deny him what every citizen is entitled to by law ... Every action of De Kom's met with a contrary action."

6 TN: Bharat Uday: An association for immigrants from British India to Suriname.

7 "We would not presume to claim that the wage decrease did not take place with the requisite tact, but we cannot escape the impression that the way it was put into practice left something to be desired" (*Algemeen Handelsblad*, July 6, 1933).

8 TN: *Echo's uit de missies* ("Echoes from the Mission") was the name of a newsletter published by Franciscan nuns from

the Netherlands who were mission workers in Suriname, but De Kom may be using the phrase more generically here.

9 TN: The exact chronology of this part of De Kom's story is difficult to follow; for a detailed account of the events with dates, see the Dutch-language biography *Anton de Kom* by Alice Boots and Rob Woortman.

10 "There was no disorderly conduct, no real opposition to the police; when they cleared the streets, of course the mood was not amicable; blows were struck by the police, which of course was inevitable" (*De Surinamer*, February 5, 1933).

11 TN: Franciscus van Haaren had been the acting governor of Suriname from October 1932 to January 1933, while Governor Abraham Rutgers was on leave.

12 "It was clear that the situation was highly unlikely to settle down until blows were struck, and that things would come to a head on Tuesday, February 7. On the evening of February 6 the necessary measures were therefore approved by myself after consultation with the chief public prosecutor and the commander of the troops, in order to uphold the authority of the regime and ensure the security of persons and goods" (government report).

13 Putscher (on p. 8 of the report on his speech) writes about this: "Despite all the painful events, some people still attempt to cover up the true cause of a discontent so powerful that the need to demonstrate defies death and bloody injury, and they try to blame it on the influence of one individual, De Kom ... But no reasonably intelligent person will swallow that. Those familiar with conditions in Suriname know better; for example, the correspondent to the *Algemeen Handelsblad* writes, 'The tragedy that ensued in a country of many alluring possibilities is not the fault of the people or of De Kom alone, but of the administration, the Europeans. And of the mother country.'

"True. That one individual, De Kom, was no more than the straw that breaks the camel's back, the spark that lights the kindling others have gathered ... And to think that some blame the global economic crisis and De Kom for the disturbances! No! The misguided economic policies of the

Surinamese administration are what gave rise to them, and if De Kom had any influence on them, even that was entirely the fault of the administration's ill-advised measures, taken in a psychosis of fear!" (p. 20).

14 "The character of public employees in Suriname was illustrated with astonishing clarity by the distasteful tactlessness of the floral tribute to the police, a festive occasion with plenty to eat and drink, held at almost exactly the same time as the corpses of the victims were being laid to rest" (Putscher, p. 8).

15 "How can those who believe in De Kom's innocence, having paid for their belief in him with two deaths, rivers of blood, and immeasurable suffering, suppress their outrage now that the administration has been forced to confess the impossibility of proving him guilty and has had no choice but to set him free, as the demonstrators had come to demand?" (Putscher, p. 6).

16 TN: "Captain" ("kapitein") is the Surinamese title for an indigenous village chief.

17 TN: *Twee Steden* appears to be the name of a publication, but this is not entirely clear.

18 TN: These were apparently two members of the Surinamese elite.

19 SAWO = Surinaamse Algemene Werkers Organisatie [General Surinamese Workers' Organization], a social democratic organization led by Louis Doedel. [TN: originally a footnote]

20 TN: The *Algemeen Handelsblad* was a Dutch newspaper with a libertarian, pro-business ideology.

Index

Index